THE MELTiNG POT
...The World in Your Kitchen

To Toni

Nadia

THE MELTiNG POT
...The World in Your Kitchen

Nadia Pendleton

PAPADAKIS PUBLISHER

Picture Credits:
Front cover: Ariffin Omar
Back flap: Rebecca Dadson (www.eyecompose.com)

Portraits for China and Persia: Ariffin Omar
Portraits for Italy, France, Caribbean, Estonia, Malaysia: Rebecca Dadson
Portraits for Ethiopia: Alexandra Papadakis

Food photography: Nadia Pendleton & Ariffin Omar
Food styling: Nadia Pendleton & Shareen Chua

We gratefully acknowledge the granting of permission to use these
images. Every reasonable attempt has been made to identify and
contact copyright holders. Any errors or omissions are inadvertent and
will be corrected in subsequent editions.

Design Director: Alexandra Papadakis
Designer: Shirlynn Chui

Editor: Sheila de Vallée

First published in 2006 by Papadakis Publisher
an imprint of New Architecture Group Ltd

16 Grosvenor Place, London SW1X 7HH
www.papadakis.net

ISBN: 1 901092 72 0

Printed and bound in Singapore

Contents

"Enjoy the journey as much as the destination" – Nadia

Introduction

Good food has been the backdrop to my life. I was brought up with the delectable fortune of having an Italian mother, whose passion for fresh ingredients and good cooking was unparalleled, and an English grandmother who taught me the humble pleasures of a great Yorkshire pudding, fairy cakes, and rhubarb crumble with custard. Together they gave me invaluable lessons in cooking and the art of cuisine from home and away. With this knowledge and understanding of food and cooking I have been given the opportunity to go beyond the boundaries of one cuisine, to explore the many delicious and fascinating ingredients, styles and dishes that exist in our modern multicultural society. What remains constant throughout this journey and my life is that the kitchen is the heart of my home; I have spent much of my life in its warmth, watching, learning, chatting and cooking.

I have experienced something 'different' throughout my life, from the ingredients in my fridge to the aromas of my kitchen. My story is not unusual. In the multicultural society that we live in today many people are brought up with one or both parents of foreign origin. I grew up going to friends' houses dining on the 'traditional' foods their parents prepared from Swedish kaviar on fresh black rye bread for breakfast to Trinidadian curry goat for dinner and the best lasagne this side of Milan. The migration of our parents and grandparents has resulted in the interaction of cultures, the exchange of ideas, and the opportunity to make strong and longlasting influences on each other. It is about time we overcame our fears, opened our eyes and arms, and enjoyed it.

We live in a melting pot of global cuisine and food culture. Bubbling away are tastes and fragrances as distinct as they are complementary. Each ingredient added to the pot does not dilute it; it strengthens it. We have the opportunity to add to our knowledge, increase our range, and broaden our understanding of ourselves and each other. Food represents nations without prejudice or stereotype, so our kitchens can become our cultural classrooms.

Although the desire to sit together to eat is universal, the culinary melting pot is not. In France, China or India, for example, pride, geography or economy interfere with the natural process of gastronomic osmosis. I live in the UK, where we are fortunate enough to have an open, accepting attitude to other national cuisines, so much so that we have adopted them amongst our favourites. Perhaps not being the world's most highly acclaimed cooks has allowed us the freedom to become the most adventurous!

It is perfectly normal for us to cook a Chinese stir fry on a Friday night, nibble some Mexican tortilla chips and guacamole while preparing Italian pasta before a Saturday night out, shamelessly indulging in a Turkish kebab on the way home then rounding off the week with 'traditional' English roast beef and gravy. We rightly defend good, old fashioned homely food, but we are able to open the door to so many different cuisines. Our corner shops, ethnic quarters and increasingly our supermarkets stock diverse ingredients, encouraging us to try our hand at something new.

This brings me on to 'fusion', something that when done well can be spectacular. Unfortunately what we usually get is 'confusion'. This is because those preparing it don't know how to treat the ingredients or how to combine and balance them; they don't know how to bring the best out of them. Menus become confused and tastes are spoilt. That is why it is so important to go back to the roots of each national cuisine, to learn the basics of ingredients and cooking from those who have had centuries of experience. Only then can we be even more adventurous in our own kitchens, move forward and increase the range of ingredients we use, the foods we know and tastes we enjoy. It will become so clear that you don't need special gadgets and gizmos to create these dishes. You can use your own pots and pans perhaps making a little change here and there to suit the ingredients you can now find easily. The result will always be fantastic.

Today, food is a major cultural issue. Like many of my peers I grew up in a time when microwaves and ready meals were launched to the masses, when fruit and vegetables began to come shrink wrapped, and when brands and supermarket price strategies rather than occasion or taste seemed to dictate what people bought. We are now living in the time of the celebrity chef and fad dietician; they tell us what to eat, how to eat and when to eat it. We are made to feel inferior if we cannot cook to restaurant standards but are castigated if we use the rich ingredients they use to pull it off; i.e. mountains of butter and piles of salt. It is no wonder some people are confused. It is time to go back to the things we learnt from people we can trust, those who have our best interests at heart. In this time of mass media and marketing we seem to have forgotten we have not lost the knowledge given to us by the most significant chefs in most of our lives – our mothers.

This book pays homage to mine, and the millions of others who produce great, authentic home cooking across the world. Women, historically the principal home cooks, have passed family recipes and culinary knowledge from generation to generation by word of mouth. Everyday cookery for humble families rather than the extravagant feasts of royalty held little interest for scholars or historians. It was a female 'chore' that until recently has gone relatively unnoticed in the grand scheme of society. This book may, I hope, redress the balance, recording what may otherwise go unwritten, and perhaps be lost in time. But this is the twenty-first century and women are not, and should not be, the only home cooks. Those who read it, male and female, can choose to pass on what they wish but armed with a more global culinary education they can at least decide how the die will be cast for the next generation.

I believe we can have the best of all worlds: the knowledge and understanding of ingredients and cuisine direct from an authentic source, but be free of the shackles of tradition and national boundaries. A Gujarati friend of mine said that her parents despaired that she and her sister were "the only two Indian girls in the restaurant who ordered chicken vindaloo with two forks". Eventually, though, they accepted it as inevitable; a new generation growing up in a different country. We can break culinary rules and regulations without scandal or scorn if we choose. It is this exercise of choice that is key.

Cooking and dining are not just about food; they are a cultural event, a celebration, a social occasion, a show of love and caring, a gift, a chance to bond with newcomers and old friends, a way of showing camaraderie. Dining on foreign food has long been the simplest and most accessible way for us to experience or 'taste' another culture. Ultimately, food brings people together and this book is a celebration of both diversity and unity.

In *The Melting Pot* I share with you the ingredients, diets, habits and etiquette that a group of women from an eclectic mix of backgrounds, some familiar some less so, have grown up with. In each chapter I examine the history and geography of a maternal cuisine, to find out where it all began, how and why things are done the way they are. I explore the flavours that make up a cuisine and the items in traditional store cupboards so that you too can create 'authentic' feasts for family and friends. With the echo of their voices throughout, I give you the chance to learn things you would normally never know unless you were born to it, details of diet, daily habits, the balancing of meals, and the dos and don'ts of dining. You will find tried and tested recipes from snacks and family favourites to full on feasts so you can expand your horizons, travel to another realm in the depths of your cupboards, and enjoy The World in Your Kitchen.

How to get the most out of The Melting Pot

I don't want to tell you how to use this book because you are all different and will approach it in whatever way suits you but there are a few things you can do to get the most out of The Melting Pot:

The introduction to each cuisine will give you a taste of the landscape, climate and culture in which a cuisine has been created. I hope this will help it come alive for you. Armed with a basic knowledge of the flavours of a particular cuisine you should then feel comfortable and confident with the food and be ready to try your hand at something new.

If you are familiar with one cuisine but are afraid to branch out into unfamiliar territory, try another nation in the same geographical area. The chances are that if you like French food you will like Estonian; if you like Thai you will like Malaysian; and if you like Indian you will like Persian. Once you know one border is nothing to worry about, move on. Hopefully your journey of discovery will not take as long as it took the original ingredients to find their way around the world.

Don't feel restricted to the meats or fish that are named in the recipes. Often the seasonings and sauces will work just as well with an alternative meat, fish or vegetable. I have given a few alternative suggestions in some recipes to help you.

If you are trying to create an impressive meal for a special occasion then check the 'lessons learnt' sections. Each nation uses food to celebrate with but the characteristics of one nation's cuisine might suit the temperament, style and grandeur of your event better than others. A Caribbean summer picnic, a Malaysian late night feast for hungry friends or an Italian roast for that family lunch are all fabulously suitable. Perhaps reserve the Ethiopian feast eaten with your hands for a night in with your lover rather than the first time you meet your future in-laws.

If you are a good cook, look at the 'contents of the store cupboard' sections and use this as a guide to create combinations for other dishes, perhaps to accompany those listed or simply to create your own. You will quickly realise how complementary the flavours of a nation are and how wide the scope for creating authentic flavours.

I am not suggesting that in order to create authentic ethnic food you need all the ingredients listed in the store cupboards; if that were the case I'd have to move to a bigger flat. The lists simply show what an authentic cook might have, bearing in mind theirs will be heavily weighted towards one or two particular cuisines. Yours will likely be more balanced.

"A little of what you fancy does you good" As I have learnt so much from mum's while writing this book it is only logical that this little gem of wisdom should come up. The reason I quote it is because I believe good food is just that – good food, so don't feel guilty after eating it. There is no need to think of meat as unhealthy or heavy or believe a little cream and butter should be off limits. Eat the best quality produce – whatever it might be, just less of it and you'll achieve a lot.

One of the main things I talk about in this book is balance, how all over the world we have created systems and diets to maintain that balance. It's not just about balancing meat carbs and veg. We'd all live in a far healthier world if we ate a wider variety of produce. When you look at the list of recipes try not to stick to chicken, cod and beef; give rabbit, red mullet or goat a try. Buy a whole chicken rather than six breasts, have some duck, mutton, veal. Variety is, after all, the spice of life.

Go on, play with your food. I don't mean throw it in the air but juggle the flavours, add a little more or a little less of some ingredients. Don't be restricted by my quantities. They are meant as a guide not the rule. Try combinations that you have never tried before and you will soon find just how much more you are enjoying your food.

Taste, taste and taste again. Don't worry if you don't have every ingredient on the list; use your taste buds to decide when something is just right. Add a little of this and a little of that and taste as you go along so you recognise the difference with or without it. In no time at all you will have tuned up your taste buds to understand balance and flavour in foods.

Relax and enjoy the journey of discovery as much as the destination.

An Italian Kitchen

Introduction to Italian Cuisine

"What is the glory of Dante compared to spaghetti?" So said Italian poet and philosopher Prezzolino in 1954. You may sneer, but unlike his works, spaghetti – and most Italian food – is immediately recognisable and accessible. It is highly appreciated all over the world for its elegant simplicity and wholesomeness.

In the ancient world authors such as Cato, Columella, and Pliny described the produce and specialities of the different regions exciting the senses of many a cook. Ancient Romans, not known for their restraint, used food to demonstrate their wealth and gorged themselves so much that some had *vomitoriums* added to their villas.

Once the Roman Empire collapsed the regions of Italy fragmented. Each region had to rely on its own natural resources rather than drawing on the produce of the whole country, and so the diet and, of course, the identity of the various regions changed. Each crafted and refined its own recipes, creating specialities and customs that remained unshared until Garibaldi united the nation just over a century ago.

The first printed cookbook is thought to have come from Italy: *De Honesta Voluptate et Veltudine* (On Right Pleasure and Good Health) written by Bartolomeo Platina in 1475.

Although captured on paper, real Italian cuisine does not come alive without an emotional and physical reaction. The Italians are one of the most outwardly emotional nations on earth, clearly evident from their profuse hand gestures when communicating, the uninhibited volume of conversations, the double or triple cheek kiss greeting, their relaxed attitude to passionate physical displays between couples in public, and the fact that men and women of all ages walk arm in arm.

Their emotional reaction to cooking and eating brings out the true flavour of the food. Italians prefer to think they live to eat not eat to live: *"Il cibo e l'essenza della vita"* (Food is the essence of life).

Italian cuisine has been influenced by many cultures. It lies at the crossroads of the Mediterranean. Invasions of Greeks, Arabs and Normans have left their mark on the south (for example, *cassata*, the familiar Sicilian ice-cream cake derived its name from *qas'at* the Arabic for a round bowl), as have the Saxons on the north.

There are also great variations resulting from climate. Foods from the northern regions suit cooler temperatures and the capricious conditions dictated by the Alps. Heavier dishes such as *risottos* and *polenta* feature frequently on the menu. Even the breads are much richer, with olive oil and rosemary-flavoured *focaccia* more common than the thin *grissini* and pizzas of the south.

Pastas and sauces, too, reflect the climate as much as the regional produce that accompanies them. Typically, pastas from northern Italy are rich in egg and usually flat, stuffed or rolled with lush fillings. In southern Italian sauces, colourful vegetables such as aubergines and courgettes predominate, but especially the *pomodoro* (the tomato, literally 'golden apple' – so called because the first tomatoes brought to Naples by traders returning from the New World were yellow).

The further south you travel the simpler and more country-like the cuisine. I mean this in the noblest sense. The abundance and freshness of local produce in the south, facilitated by the favourable Mediterranean climate, meant that there was little need for preserving, flavouring or enriching foods so that there would be ample supplies for difficult times.

The produce with which we are familiar is often synonymous with the region that historically produced it: Piedmontese mushrooms, Genovese *pesto*, the white truffles of Alba, *panforte* from Siena, Ligurian honey, the *gorgonzola* and *bel paese* cheeses of Lombardy, Trentino *speck* (cured meat), Parma hams, Umbrian *porchetta* (suckling pig), Roman *saltimbocca*, Apulian *orechiette*, Neopolitan pizzas and Sicilian *limoncello* to name but a few. The regions are still fiercely competitive when it comes to food production. Not such a bad thing for the export market because you are almost as likely to find a specialist southern Italian sauce at a delicatessen in Britain as you are in northern Italy.

Travel and trade played a great role not only in the spread of regional cuisines within Italy after re-unification but in the types of Italian food we know, and love, outside Italy. It was not the aristocracy who popularised this cuisine as was the case in France but the mass of workers, especially those from the south, who fled Italy to make their fortunes abroad. They took with them the recipes and memories of their mother's staple foods: hearty meat and fish stews, fresh pasta and simple pizzas. This *cucina povera* (rustic food) is incredibly popular all over the world.

Brought together, the ingredients and styles from all parts of Italy complement each other beautifully and are restricted only by the imagination of the cook or those dining on Italy's delicious dishes.

Flavours of an Italian Kitchen

When people think of Italy they often think in the colours of the Italian flag: plump, red, sun-ripened tomatoes; clean, silky-white mozzarella; and fragrant, fresh, green basil. These staples represent the cuisine well and highlight the importance of freshness, simple local produce and seasoning with the lightest touch of fresh herbs. Herbs play a vital role in creating the subtle flavours of Italian cuisine. Sage, rosemary, thyme and mint, freshly cut from the garden, add clarity and aroma. Spices, too, play their part: saffron stems stored in little pots give warmth and colour; red chilli for bite and fire; star anise and cloves for a touch of the bitter sweet. Lemons emphasise freshness and, of course, the vast array of seasonal forest mushrooms and truffles add depth and richness.

As a child I spent almost every holiday back in Italy. We packed light because when we returned to England our bags would be laden with as many authentic food products as possible — olive oils, wine and balsamic vinegars, huge bricks of Parmigiano Reggiano, stock cubes and powders, dried mushrooms and truffles, along with polenta and risotto rice.

Olive oils are extremely important in most regional Italian cooking with varieties ranging from strong, cold-pressed, unfiltered extra-virgin oil to the mellower filtered 'second press' oils, early harvest and late harvest oils, and infused or flavoured oils. Each has its purpose and distinctive flavour. Dark green extra-virgin oils are best to dress foods such as salads, pasta or risotto. Virgin is often used to brown meats and cook hot-pot dishes; milder golden blended oils are more suitable for deep frying. Like fine wines, olive oil should be stored in dark bottles away from direct sunlight. Unlike some rustic produce, sediment in the bottle does not necessarily mean a more 'authentic' or better quality oil but rather that

it has been exposed to heat on its journey. Also, as with wine, you will find some oils suit your palate better than others. There are many ways to judge the quality of an olive oil, most seem fruity at first but this flavour dies down after a couple of mouthfuls in a poorer quality oil. Look out for peppery, musky, green grass tones with hints of melon, hay and nuts – all good flavours to find in olive oil.

Mamma came over to the UK from Bergamo in the north of Italy in 1969 after being whisked off her feet by her English teacher, my Dad. From a world of spam and potatoes his culinary world was changed for life. When I think of Bergamascan food and my mother's Italian cooking it's not the vision presented on TV or even on the supermarket shelves. I think alpine food, rich with cured and roasted meats, thick yellow polenta, risottos and a myriad of cheeses.

The northern Italian climate has always been too hostile for olive trees, and so for centuries they turned to dairy produce in the north. Butter and cream are still used in many more regional dishes than in the south, as are matured cheeses. Nutty, flaky Parmesan, notably that from the Reggiano region, is central to many weekly meals. Blue cheeses such as *dolcelatte* and *gorgonzola* add piquancy and are just as good cooked as fresh. Powdery *ricotta* and creamy *mascarpone* cheeses are ideal for baking and desserts.

Italian rice, the staple of the north, originates mainly from the Po valley. It has a noble history. Once used to feed the gladiators in Rome, it was so prized that the authorities had to step in to cap it at twelve gold imperials a pound. Today, there are three main types of rice grain used in Italian cooking: *arborio* – the most common in British supermarkets, *carnaroli* and *vialone nano*, all more reasonably priced. *Arborio* is high in starch content, which thickens with cooking whilst the grain retains its bite. *Carnaroli* has a shorter grain, producing the firm, balanced consistency perfect for creamy risottos; *vialone nano*, a stubby grain with rounded edges is robust and favoured for garnished risottos.

Pasta originates from the south of Italy or from China depending how far back in history you look. It is now the mainstay of Italian cuisine, each type created with aesthetic flair and practical purpose. Thick sauces are used with fatter pasta, such as *rigatoni*, or *papardelle*, or the more contoured shapes; while thinner pasta, like *spaghetti*, which are easily coated, are served with oily or liquid sauces. Fresh pasta is perfect for shaping, stuffing and filling, while dried is more suitable for soups; it stands up to the heat better in bakes and the texture complements 'soft' foods like fish and seafood.

Mamma's favourite story about settling down in England sums up an Italian's love of pasta and ragú. "I remember going to see an Edoardo de Filippo play at the Old Vic. Laurence Olivier, his wife and Peppino de Filippo were in it. It was a story about a woman who prepared some ragú and the events that went on around her as it bubbled away on the stove. They were actually cooking this ragú on stage and the smell was incredible. I was there with Bambina, a friend from home and we had really only just arrived. We were hungry because we did not have that much money and there was not much food around in those days. As the ragú started to cook we were mesmerised, salivating. I can't remember what went on in the play but the smell of the ragú will remain with me forever.

Today, it is easier than ever to find high quality authentic Italian products from *sott'olio* to *prosciutto crudo* and a vast array of artisanal, local products. These have

thankfully replaced the over-seasoned, bitter tomato sauces and bland pastas of yesteryear.

Contents of an Italian Store Cupboard

<u>Dried Pasta</u>:
Variety of Flat, Fat, Thin, Shaped

Polenta
Arborio and *Carnaroli* Rice
Dried Breadcrumbs
Vegetable, Veal and Chicken Stock
Oregano
Parsley
Basil
Rosemary
Sage
Thyme

Saffron
Nutmeg
Lemons
Garlic
Pesto
Tomato Passata (Sieved Tomato)
Tomato Purée
Sun Dried Tomatoes
Parmesan
Pecorino (Hard Goat's Cheese)
Pancetta
Olives
Anchovies
Capers
Dried Porcini Mushrooms
Mushrooms in Oil

Artichokes in Oil
Peppers in Oil
Onions
Courgettes
Aubergines
Potatoes
Fagioli beans
Lentils

<u>Olive Oil</u>:
Light and Extra Virgin

Red and White Wine
Red and White Wine Vinegar
Balsamic Vinegar
Marsala
Amaretto
Grappa

Lessons learnt along the way...

Dining habits prove to be the strongest traditions, persisting when other aspects of culture have disappeared. The Mediterranean diet has long been praised for its contribution to a healthy heart and long life. Its principles are simple: eat fresh, balanced meals and don't snack. If you look at Italian foods there are few snacks because Italians favour long drawn-out meals that are satisfying enough to carry you through to the next one.

The Italians are as strict with their diet as they are with fashion and my mother was no exception.

Coffee is as essential to diet as the little black dress is to an Italian woman's wardrobe. For adults the day starts with a stimulant-rich breakfast to buzz through the morning; a *cappuccino* or *espresso* served *corto* (short, with very little water passed through the coffee at great pressure) or *lungo* (a longer coffee with a shot's worth of water), accompanied by a sweet pastry. Children have a bowl of hot milk or cocoa and a few biscuits or cereal. A *caffè americano* (a big cup of filter coffee is usually reserved for the afternoons, if ever).

My alarm was the sound of the caffettiera bubbling on the stove and the smell of fresh coffee wafting up the stairs. My parents drank their shots of thick silky lavazza while I tucked into my cereal. This habit is one I have adopted with pleasure.

Lunch is the most important meal of the day: protein rich, wholesome and filling. Unfortunately, modern working habits don't allow for three-hour lunches but in Italy there is still a second rush hour to get home for *mezzogiorno* (midday). Meals should be eaten at a leisurely pace with portions that are relatively small, so that they can be digested and perhaps followed by a *pisolino* (nap) before the return to work.

Most importantly, whenever you eat, *"Si lascia la tavola con un po di appetito"* (you must leave the table with a little bit of appetite). After all, to enjoy a glass of wine space must be left at the top for the flavours to develop!

Merenda, like English teatime, is enjoyed mid-afternoon. It is considered the most appropriate time for a *caffè latte*, *cioccolata* or *té* with lemon. This would be accompanied by a *merendina* – chocolate, a sweet pastry, or a biscuit. Dinner is served later and lighter: most often a small pasta or soup followed by hams, some cheese and salad with (often disappointingly for some children) fruit or yogurt to finish.

When I was growing up I loved going over to friends' houses for dinner. I thought the food was great. I'd try foods like chicken nuggets and Findus crispy pancakes, and things we didn't have in our house, like crisps and orange squash, but would most look forward to puddings like jam roly-poly and custard or butterscotch angel delight – heavenly. It's incredible how things change.

Whatever goes on the table, Italians eat together at every meal. Dinner is an important time for families to relax, share stories, news and views:

The kitchen table was, and still is, the heart of family life. We grew up together round the table...having fights, having laughs, good times, bad times, big disappointments, big announcements, always round the kitchen table.

If there is anything to celebrate – and Italians need very little excuse to do so – they also take to the table. This is not always a family affair. Even today people say, *"Natale con i tuoi, Pasqua con chi vuoi"* (Christmas with your own and Easter with whomever you please).

This is a good way of encouraging groups of friends to get together for a feast.

A celebration meal is always a big event and would normally consist of some seven courses. It is customary never to arrive at someone's home empty handed. A beautifully wrapped tray of sweet delicacies is often given in place of flowers or wine when invited to lunch or dinner.

Before the meal starts you are welcomed by the host, even if it is just family, with an *apperitivo*, usually dry cocktails to whet the appetite such as Campari, dry Martini or an *analcolico* (a non-alcoholic dry drink such as *Crodino* or *San Bitter*). These are accompanied by a few savoury, bread-based nibbles such as *grissini*, *crostini* or *bruschetta*. The hot *apperitivi* are always served before the cold ones. The host always proposes the first toast *(Salute)* to get the fun and -eating under way. It is important to make eye contact with all the people you toast individually, rather than looking at their glasses. Although this might lead to a few spilt drops it is very bad manners, bad luck (or bad sex as young Italians usually say) not to look people in the eye.

The courses are always served in the same order:

Antipasto – large platters of rich cured meats, hams and salamis, olives, anchovies, colourful *sott'olio* or *sott'aceto* vegetables glistening amongst them, passed round convivially and accompanied by an abundance of fresh bread. The *antipasti* awaken the taste buds and start the juices flowing.

Primo – either a pasta or rice course is always served as a separate course rather than an accompaniment. For a more elaborate meal such as a wedding or Christmas there is often a second *primo* usually a

delicate, beautiful terrine, pâté or mousse crafted to prepare the mind as well as the palate for the courses to come.

Pesce – the fish or seafood course is served with a few vegetables or alone.

Secondo – the main meat course comes with *contorni* (side dishes of potatoes and other vegetables)

Formaggi – cheeses are served with grapes or pear and dried fruits, rather than crackers or bread.

Frutta – fresh fruit is laid out in bowls and on platters to refresh the palate and rest the stomach before the rich finale

Dolci – desserts do not feature as heavily in the daily Italian diet as the British but on special occasions the rich, cream-based desserts with which we are familiar – *tiramisu*, *pannacotta* or *zabaglione* – are served.

Coffee may not count as a course but it follows every meal. The Italians would never dream of serving a *caffè latte* or *cappuccino* after a meal, not just because it is considered bad etiquette but because hot milk blocks the stomach and hinders digestion, which is unwise after such feasting. *Espresso* is served with a crunchy *cantuccini* or *amaretto* biscuit and a digestive liqueur such as *limoncello* or *amaro* (a stronger version of *amaretto*).

When it comes to Italian food there is a simple adage: *"I cose si fan' bene, o non si fanno"* (do it well or don't do it at all). This applies not only to cooking and eating but the way you behave at table. There are many unspoken rules: eating lots of bread, which is served with all main meals, is reserved for children and young men with large appetites. You should never scrape the plate with your cutlery but you may wipe it with bread when you are at home with the family. Never cut pasta or suck it into your mouth. Not being able to twist longer pasta using your fork at the side of the bowl but needing a spoon is considered childish. Greediness can still provoke contempt amongst many Italians, stemming from its inclusion as one of the seven deadly sins in the Catholic religion. Eating too fast also insults the host as you would not show you appreciate the effort and time that went into cooking. You should never need to do either as you will never go short of food in an Italian household:

Good hosts always offer more than you could ever eat. They feel it is their duty. My mother still lists the contents of the fruit bowl, the fridge and her cupboards searching for something else she can offer me at the end of the meal to ensure I have had enough. She knows I'll say no to everything but it is in her nature to do so. It still makes me laugh.

All that said and done, if you are in the company of a group of Italians enjoying a meal you would not notice any of this above the din of the conversation and the boisterous gesticulating of your fellow diners (and neither would they).

When we were children Nonno, my grandfather, used to say, "Buon appetito, mangia e fa' sito". This was Bergamascan dialect for "Enjoy your meal, eat and be quiet"...He meant it affectionately, of course, because he knew the quiet would last about thirty seconds

Italian holidays are easily defined by different foods – especially cakes. At Easter there is *colomba*, a light cake encrusted with sugar and almonds in the shape of a dove to represent peace. At Christmas *panettone*, a fruity, bread-like cake is given to friends and family members

alongside gifts. New Year is commemorated with a *pan d'oro*, a golden cake sometimes filled with chocolate or liqueur creams, shaped like a tall tower and dusted with white icing sugar, a tradition started in the patrician families of the Veneto region. Finally, good fortune in the New Year can be guaranteed by a more savoury option: *lenticchie* (lentils) served with *zampone*, *cotecchino* or other large sausages. Like rice in China, lentils represent riches to the Italians; the more you eat, the more riches you will have in the following year.

Like many beliefs and rituals that surround Italy and its cuisine, the superstitions have faded; the food has travelled far and wide but the traditions stand firm.

Tortelli di Zucca al Burro e Salvia
Pumpkin Tortelli with Butter and Sage

Tortelli are round like a torta or cake. Making them with two discs of pasta means you can add a lot of filling to each tortelli. If you prefer smaller pasta, simply use half the amount of filling and fold each disc of pasta over the filling to make a half-moon. As your fork slides through the pasta, the orange glow of pumpkin and the dark green of the crisp sage make a great contrast and give an incredible texture. Once you have made fresh pasta a couple of times there is no turning back.

I always use fresh organic free-range eggs. The yolks are incredibly rich and yellow, so different from shop-bought eggs. With only three ingredients in pasta the quality of each makes a real difference. The good thing is that none of them is expensive if you think how much end-product you can make with a little time and effort.

I wouldn't be truly Italian if pasta wasn't on my list of favourite dishes. It is one of the best fast foods available on the market and good for the whole family. There are thousands of types of pasta, each with an individual flavour and purpose, but there is no reason why that should intimidate you. I have given you the first recipe of an Italian kitchen: fresh pasta. If you make it once you will find yourself hooked for ever. Of course there is nothing wrong with a packet of dried spaghetti and a bag of fusilli to keep you going on a day-to-day basis. Just don't mention it to a local Italian who would have you believe that you were poisoning yourself if you were to combine the wrong pasta with the wrong sauce or, heaven forbid, not cook it in the most traditional way. They can be frustratingly stubborn. Luckily, I can choose to bring out the English half of me when these lectures begin. Instead of chastising me, I think they begin to pity me. Either way it works to get them off my case and on to the cooking.

This recipe reminds me of autumn nights. Mamma would send me out in the dark and freezing cold to get some fresh sage from the garden. Stepping back into the warmth and seeing the steam rising from the pan heightened my appetite and readied my taste buds.

For the filling:

1 medium pumpkin	Black pepper
Salt to taste	50g white breadcrumbs
250g parmesan cheese	Flour for dusting
70g butter	A glug of olive oil
3 eggs	3 sage leaves
½ tsp freshly ground nutmeg	

PREP:

1 Peel, scrape out seeds and fibrous middle section of the pumpkin and discard. Chop the flesh into large chunks

2 Place the pumpkin in a pan with enough cold water to cover it. Bring to the boil, salt liberally, cook for 30 minutes or until a knife passes through the flesh without too much resistance

3 Meanwhile grate the cheese and set aside

4 Drain off the water. Add a large knob of butter (about 20g) and mash the pumpkin

5 Whisk 2 eggs and add to the mashed pumpkin along with the nutmeg and a few twists of black pepper

6 Add 200g of the parmesan and the breadcrumbs so that the filling mix is fairly dry but not solid. Taste and adjust seasoning

7 Use a pasta machine or roll out the pasta on a lightly floured surface to 2mm thick. Use a glass or pastry cutter to cut circles

8 Place a teaspoonful of filling in the middle of each circle, whisk the other egg and dab a little with a pastry brush or your finger around the edges of the pasta

9 Place another disc over the top; seal at two opposite points, then pick it up in your hand and work the two pieces of pasta together round the filling, pinching the edges together tightly. Make sure the air is squeezed out around the filling so that it will not burst in the water

TIP:
Wash the pumpkin seeds you have removed and spread them out on a baking tray. Next time the oven is on put them in and roast them for about 20 minutes with a little salt or sugar for a healthy snack or salad topping.

COOK:

1. Bring a large pan of water to a rolling boil, salt liberally and add a glug of oil. This will reinforce the pasta and stop the tortelli from sticking together

2. Spoon in the *tortelli*. They will cook in approximately 4 minutes. Turn the pan from side to side to release any that may have stuck and keep an eye on it in case you have to rescue any that have opened and might leak and stick to each other

3. Before serving, melt a large knob of butter (about 50g) in a small pan

4. Add the fresh sage leaves and cook until the leaves are crisp and the butter foams. Be careful to take the pan off the heat just before the butter blackens

5. Pour the melted butter and crisp sage over the *tortelli* and cover generously with the remaining 50g of freshly grated parmesan. Serve immediately

For the *Pasta all'Uovo*:

200g '00' type flour (50g per person)	2 large eggs
	A large pinch of salt

PREP:

1 Create a well in the sifted flour, crack in the eggs and add a large pinch of salt

2 Gradually work in the flour towards the middle of the well using your fingers, then blend to a dough. If it is too sticky add more flour, a good pinch at a time. If it is too dry add more water, a tablespoon at a time. Knead until smooth

3 Let the dough rest for at least 15 minutes

Gnocchi di Noci ai Quattro Formaggi [Walnut Gnocchi with Four Cheese Sauce]

Gnocchi di Noci ai Quattro Formaggi

Walnut Gnocchi with Four Cheese Sauce

Usually made of potato, flour, water and a little salt, *gnocchi* are filling and, dressed simply, very healthy.

If you buy the plain gnocchi this dish is extremely fast to whip up. You don't need to stand over it for hours so it is perfect for an impromptu dinner party after five minutes preparation in the kitchen you can be the perfect hostess/host chatting to your guests while the cheeses bubble away under the grill, creating a rich, luxurious dish. These quantities make an excellent starter for six or stand-alone main course for four.

For the gnocchi:		
20 walnuts	1kg white potatoes	1 egg
Salt		200g plain flour
For the sauce:		
50g gorgonzola	50g emmental	Handful of chives
50g parmesan	50g fontina	Knob of butter

PREP:

1 Shell the walnuts and crush them in a pestle and mortar or in the coffee-grinder of a blender to make a smooth, fine flour

2 Boil the potatoes until a knife passes through easily, then peel

3 While they are still warm pass them through a ricer into a bowl or mash them well

4 Add a generous pinch of salt and one beaten egg

5 Add the walnut flour, then, gradually, the plain flour so that the paste becomes elastic and firm. If the mixture is too dry add an additional spoonful of beaten egg. Too much flour and the gnocchi become hard, too little and they break up in the pan

6 To shape the gnocchi roll the paste out into a sausage then pinch off a piece the size of the end of your thumb

7 To add texture to the gnocchi so that they absorb more sauce, make small little indentations on top with the back of a fork.

COOK:

1. Bring a pan of water to the boil, salt liberally and throw in the gnocchi. Within 3-4 minutes they will rise to the surface. Allow them to simmer for no longer than 6 minutes

2. Meanwhile, grate the parmesan, fontina and emmental. Cut the gorgonzola into small pieces. Using a warm knife will make this easier and cleaner; you can dip the blade into the water in which the gnocchi are boiling

3. Drain the gnocchi and place them in an ovenproof serving dish

4. Quickly stir in a knob of butter, then sprinkle over the fontina, emmental, gorgonzola and chopped chives

5. Bake in a moderate oven for 5 minutes so that the cheeses melt and blend together. Stir to make sure all the *gnocchi* are covered in cheese, sprinkle with parmesan to make a delicious crust that will add texture to the dish. Return to the oven for 5 minutes

Mamma recalls her brother and sister joining her and her mother at the kitchen table to roll the gnocchi. In a flurry of hand movements her mother would pinch off a piece of the dough thrusting it towards each child in turn. Each would use the back of a fork to make the little indentations, before piling them onto the floured board at the end of the table. A batch of a hundred gnocchi would fly out in minutes.

Risotto alla Milanese

Milanese Style Saffron Risotto

1 shallot	1 glass good quality dry white wine
80g butter	3-4 saffron stems or 1 tsp saffron powder
Splash of extra virgin olive oil	Parmesan (to taste)
350g *arborio* or *carnaroli* rice	
1 litre vegetable or chicken stock	

This dish typifies Italian cooking in my eyes: it is both simple and stylish. The Italians have a way of making very few ingredients marry so well together in a dish that the flavours take on a wonderful depth and intensity. This *risotto* is light enough to enjoy in the summer and the saffron gives it that warm glow that makes it comforting and warming in winter.

It is imperative that you use a risotto rice such as *arborio* or *carnaroli* because the water swells the short fat grains from the inside, while the outside of the grain softens slowly releasing the starch that gives the characteristic creamy texture. Long grain, Thai fragrant and basmati rice are all too delicate, cook too quickly, and turn into rice-mush (or congee) if overcooked. When you fork through the *risotto* you should be able to see the separate grains and still feel the texture. Many people assume that the characteristic texture of a *risotto* is achieved by adding cream, which is not the case. A knob of butter is added once the *risotto* is cooked (called *mantecare il risotto*). This glazes the rice and adds richness to the already creamy *risotto*. The parmesan balances this creaminess with its natural saltiness, nuttiness and piquancy.

If you are using fresh saffron for the first time you may be surprised at how much colour and aroma come from one or two 'threads' and you may find your fingers, chopping board, wooden spoon and other utensils keep the colour for a long time. A really effective way to clean them (and your inevitably yellow pan) is to rub them all over with a freshly cut lemon.

PREP:

1 Finely chop shallots

2 Warm the stock or prepare with stock cubes and boiling water

COOK:

1. In a pan melt 50g butter and a dash of olive oil. Add the shallot and cook over a low heat until translucent

2. Add the rice and stir to coat each grain in the butter; add a ladle of prepared stock, a glass of white wine and stir until the liquid has almost evaporated and the rice takes on a nice sheen

3. Continue to add ladles of stock, one at a time, until half the stock has been used and the rice is plump

4. Add the saffron to the final quarter of the stock and keep stirring the risotto. Taste and adjust seasoning. The rice should still have a bite to it but the whole risotto should be creamy. Add more stock as necessary.

5. Take the rice off the heat, stir in the remaining 30g of butter. Sprinkle with grated parmesan cheese and serve

TIP:

If you have left over risotto a good way to use it up is to roll it into balls and fill them with a lump of *mozzarella* (not *mozzarella di bufala*, which is too soft and delicate) or a spoonful of *Bolognese* sauce. Roll the balls in egg wash, then breadcrumbs, and fry them to make a delicious snack called *arancini di riso* (rice oranges).

Torta di Spinaci
Spinach Pie

The ham in this pie smells wonderfully sweet when cooked and the mozzarella oozes out when you open up the pastry. It is a complete meal and something that can be rustled up really easily. This is the perfect recipe when people drop in unexpectedly. Using frozen pastry means that little preparation time is needed and the result is so impressive that everyone thinks you have been slaving away for hours.

500g spinach	A knob of butter
2 eggs	1 tbsp flour
1 large ball mozzarella	Salt and pepper
5 thick slices cooked ham	Freshly grated nutmeg (to taste)
250g puff pastry	

PREP:

1 Wash and steam the spinach for 4-5 minutes until the leaves have wilted. If you buy it in a cellophane bag, you can microwave it unopened for 4 minutes

2 Drain well, squeezing out as much water as possible. You can do this by wrapping the spinach in a clean tea towel and wringing it out until no more water escapes, or by just squeezing it into a sieve with your hands. It may feel as if you are losing the bulk of the spinach but any remaining water will sit in the pie and make the crusts soggy if this is not done properly

3 Whisk the eggs

4 Chop the ham and mozzarella into small pieces

5 Roll out the puff pastry in 2 sheets

6 Butter and lightly flour a baking tin or ovenproof dish

COOK:

1. Cover the base and up to the rim of an ovenproof dish with a layer of pastry

2. Put the chopped ham and mozzarella onto the base. Putting them at the bottom helps keep any moisture released by the spinach away from the crust

3. Pour over half the beaten egg and finally the spinach

4. Season well with salt, pepper and nutmeg

5. Cover with the second sheet of pastry. Roll the edges together to seal. Trim the sides and decorate with any remaining strips of pastry

6. Brush the top with the remaining whisked egg

7. Place in the oven on the middle shelf at 200°C for 35-40 minutes until the pastry has turned golden brown. Serve hot or cold

When our daffodils came out, when the grass in the garden was thick and I had given up chocolate for Lent (again!) I knew spring was well and truly upon us. Another sign was the fabulous spinach pie my mother used to make. We'd go to the market and buy two enormous carrier bags full of fresh spinach, which would almost magically shrink to end up in one pie.

Lasagne alla Bolognese
Bolognese Style Lasagne

There are lots of different styles of *lasagne*: *pasticcera* is a white lasagne made with veal and ham; *lasagne di funghi* is made simply with mushrooms and cream. This recipe is for the classic well-known and well-loved dish from Bologna. The *ragú* is basically the *Bolognese* sauce that foreigners eat more commonly with spaghetti. *Bolognese* sauce is better served with a fatter, heavier pasta that picks up more sauce and so *lasagne* is perfect. There are a few things that make a difference when making *lasagne*: one is slow cooking the *ragú* for as long as possible to intensify the flavours; the other is to have a perfect *besciamella*. Many people omit the cooking time of the *besciamella* but this is vital, not only so that you don't get indigestion from the raw flour but to ensure that the sauce isn't pasty and bland. One last thing: Italians hate to see fresh salad served on the same plate as hot *ragú*. Each spoils the taste and texture of the other. A salad accompani-ment should be served on a side plate.

Dried *lasagne* sheets in a packet are fine and no longer need to be pre-cooked but you can now buy fresh pasta sheets from many stores. If you prefer to start from scratch, use my basic *pasta all'uovo* recipe.

Homemade *pasta all'uovo* or 1 packet of dried pasta sheets	200ml passata di pomodoro
For the *ragú*:	1/2 tube tomato purée
1 large onion	Salt and pepper
1 large carrot	1 large pinch of oregano
2 sticks of celery	For the *besciamella*:
1 clove garlic	Parmesan cheese, grated
3 glugs virgin olive oil	50g butter
500g lean minced prime beef	50g flour
1 large glass red wine	500ml cold milk
225 ml beef or veal stock	1 tsp freshly grated nutmeg
	Grated parmesan to taste

I remember when I was a kid the smell of the rich ragú would fill the house for a day. I can still see my mother in a steamy kitchen cooking the freshly rolled sheets of pasta and laying them on a tea-towel to dry. She'd then switch round to whisking the besciamella and grating in sweet smelling nutmeg. I used to steal the stock cube wrappers and suck them to get the salty flavour. After hours on the stove everything would come together, the anticipation almost unbearable, the result always spectacular.

<u>PREP:</u>

1 Dice the onion, carrot and celery into small pieces

2 Peel the garlic

<u>COOK:</u>

1. First make the *soffritto* by heating the olive oil in a large pot and adding the thinly diced carrots, celery and onions with a whole clove of garlic. Allow them to soften and caramelize slightly

2. Add the seasoned minced meat to the *soffritto* and brown well

3. Pour in the glass of wine, stirring gently. Allow it to evaporate over a medium heat

4. Add the beef or veal stock, the *passata* and the tomato purée and stir. Taste and season with salt, pepper and oregano. Cover the pot and allow the *ragú* to simmer on a low heat for at least 40 minutes, stirring occasionally. If you have a diffuser you can keep it cooking slowly for up for 4 hours, which really does intensify the flavours. But keep an eye on it and add stock if required as moisture is necessary to keep the pasta soft and the whole dish together

5. If using fresh pasta, roll out on a well floured surface and cut into rectangles the size of the dish you will be using. approximately as wide and as long as your hand. Make sure the sheets fit with no gaps at the sides. Cover with a clean, damp cloth until ready to use

6. Just before the *ragú* is cooked bring a pan of salted water to the boil and drop in the lasagne sheets. Cook for 3 minutes, remove and lay them on clean tea towels, cover with more clean, damp tea-towels until you are ready to assemble the layers

7. For the *besciamella*, melt the butter in a heavy based pan. Mix in the flour, little by little, stirring constantly to make a thick paste. The trick to keeping the sauce lump free is speed and strength. Have the milk ready in a small jug rather than pouring from a big bottle. At first add it glug by glug working each glug into the butter/flour paste completely before adding the next. Once you have used about one third of the milk you should have a creamy consistency and can free-flow the rest slowly but continuously. Season with salt

8. Let the mixture come to the boil then turn the heat down and simmer for 15 minutes, stirring occasionally, to cook the flour through. The sauce should sit on the back of a spoon and not drip when you draw a finger through it

9. The final, essential touch to any *besciamella* is to add freshly grated nutmeg to taste

10. Spoon a little *ragú* into an ovenproof dish, cover with a layer of pasta. Continue with layers of *ragú*, pasta and *besciamella* until all the *ragú* is used up. The top layer should be *besciamella*. Grate a little parmesan on top

11 Cover in foil and bake for 35 minutes at 200°C. Remove the foil, grate more parmesan over the *lasagne* and return to the oven to brown for another 6 or 7 minutes. Slice and serve

Polenta con Coniglio e Funghi Selvatici
Polenta with Herb Roasted Rabbit and Wild Mushrooms

Polenta is a regional speciality from Bergamo in the Lombardy region of northern Italy. The artisanal style old-fashioned polenta had to be stirred constantly with a wooden *mescola* until you felt that your arm would drop off. It was cooked over an open fire in a copper pot with a round base. Nowadays, there are still round- bottomed polenta pots but the variety of quick-cook polenta means that it can be prepared in as little as 6 minutes.

Polenta can be served with a multitude of things in a multitude of ways: piled high with *osei* (whole roasted sparrows), fried with fat sausages, griddled with cheese and vegetables, or wrapped round gorgonzola and baked. Quick-cook polenta should be prepared just a few minutes before time as it hardens fast and is then difficult to pour and mould.

This herb roasted rabbit with wild forest mushrooms is one of my favourite dishes. The rich juices of the meat ooze over the top of the bright yellow mountain of polenta like an erupting volcano and the

mushrooms lend themselves well to the earthy, gamey meat. Rabbit is delicious and used to be popular for everyday meals. When ordering it you should ask your butcher for one aged between three months and a year, any older and the meat is too tough, any younger and there is not enough meat. When cooking rabbit the most important consideration is that it dries out easily but if you cover it, baste and baste again, you will be well rewarded with the most delicious meat.

This was Mamma's favourite dish when she was growing up. When I asked her about it not long ago she said, "I can still smell it and taste it. We used to go to the mountains in the summer for a month and my father would come up every Sunday carrying a gâteau of dry ice that he used to buy at the bottom of the hill. It was 30°C so we needed to keep cool. We'd go out to the yard and choose the rabbit we wanted to eat and my grandfather would kill it. We didn't have the same sensibilities back then; this was the country and animals were raised to be eaten. Everyone kept rabbits and chickens, some even had pigs in their backyards and they would be fed on grain and nuts from the woods. When it was time to start cooking the children had the privilege of choosing which rabbit we would eat. We never saw it killed. The next thing we knew it was on the table. The amazing thing was cooking the polenta on the open fire in August when it was 30°C and we were all sweating away round an open fire. We sat there preparing the mushrooms we had picked in the woods that day too. The memory will always stay with me. Cuisine at its very best."

1 medium rabbit	A handful of thyme
1 litre of water	A handful of sage
1 cup white wine vinegar	3 cloves of garlic
2 handfuls of dried porcini mushrooms	Olive oil
	200g + 50g butter
2 handfuls of button mushrooms	150ml chicken stock
	300ml dry white wine
2 handfuls of baby chestnut mushrooms	Polenta: 120g per person to 350ml of water
Salt and pepper	
2 sprigs of rosemary	A handful of parsley

PREP:

1 Prepare the rabbit by soaking it in 1 litre of water and a cup of vinegar for about 30 minutes, then rinse and dry

2 Soak the dried porcini mushrooms in warm water for at least 10 minutes. Any dirt or grit will settle to the bottom of the bowl so rather than draining them in a colander and mixing the grit back in, lift out the mushrooms with a slotted spoon

3 Take the butter out of the fridge so it is at room temperature Clean and slice the fresh mushrooms and set aside

4 Pre-heat the oven to 180°C

COOK:

1. Season the rabbit inside and out and stuff it with half the rosemary, thyme and sage, a large knob of butter (about 50g), and 2 garlic cloves halved

2. Place in an ovenproof dish and brush it all over with a little olive oil

3. Put on the hob and brown all over then spread the remaining butter (150g) and herbs over the skin. Pour over 200ml wine and 150ml stock

4. Cover with foil and place in the oven for 1¼ hours (depending on the size of the rabbit). Turn half way through cooking and if the flesh looks dry add a few more tablespoons of stock or warm water

5. To prepare the polenta bring the water to the boil adding a generous pinch of salt. Pour in the *polenta* and stir quickly until all the water is absorbed. Simmer for 45 minutes (for quick cook polenta follow the guidelines on the packet) stirring in one direction, as continuously as your arm allows. When it has reached the consistency of a thick mash and comes away from the sides of the pan it is ready

6. Cook the mushrooms by melting 50g of butter and two glugs of olive oil in a pan. Add one whole peeled clove of garlic and wait for the aroma to hit you. When it does, the pan is ready for the mushrooms. Fry them gently and once they have taken on a little colour, add a small glass of dry white wine (100ml) and a little stock (about 50ml). Turn up the heat and fry for 10-15 minutes

7. Towards the end of cooking the mushrooms, finely chop a handful of fresh parsley and throw in the pan, tossing and heating through

8. When the rabbit is cooked allow it to rest for at least 10 minutes, then joint it, separating the front and back legs and cutting the back section into 3 pieces. Return the pieces to the roasting dish along with the juices and keep warm while you plate the polenta

9. To present the dish, take a large platter and pour out the polenta so that it creates a wide volcano. Pile the mushrooms in the crater and lay the rabbit pieces on top, spooning over the juices. Take to the table and slice each portion ensuring each person has a piece of everything. Alternatively, you can make smaller volcanoes on each plate and serve

Melanzane Impannate [Aubergine in Breadcrumbs]

Melanzane Impannate
Aubergine in Breadcrumbs

This is by far my favourite way to eat aubergines: crunchy on the outside and smooth on the inside. Too often aubergines are cooked badly, leaving people with the impression that they are rubbery or bland. Prepared this way they melt in the mouth with a sweetness and succulence that is second to none.

Salting the aubergines is important as it takes away their bitter taste; frying them when they are too thick or wet makes the fritters soggy. The salt should be coarse as the larger granules draw the moisture out of the flesh of the aubergine without being absorbed as quickly as fine salt. The slices should be fairly thin as you want them to cook through before the breadcrumbs burn, but not so thin that they absorb too much oil and shrivel into nothing. It is also important that you do not cover the cooked fritters to keep them warm as the steam escaping from the cooked aubergines will be trapped and the condensation will turn the crispy breadcrumbs soggy. Much better to put the whole dish in a warm oven. A small warning: cooking a batch of them leads to a smoky kitchen, so keep the windows open.

These fritters are delicious with a salad or served with grilled chicken or fish as part of a picnic lunch.

2 large aubergines (1/2 per person)	200g breadcrumbs (from a dried baguette or ciabatta loaf)
A handful of coarse sea salt	Light olive or seed oil for frying
2 eggs	

PREP:

1 Slice the aubergines lengthways, about 1/2cm thick

2 Put them on a clean tea towel and sprinkle a handful of coarse sea salt over them. When water droplets form on top of the slices (about 10 minutes), rinse them under cold water to remove the salt. Wipe dry with kitchen paper

3 Whisk the egg and season it with a little salt and pepper

COOK:

1. Prepare your production line: a bowl of whisked egg, a plate with the breadcrumbs on it, and a plate ready for the fried aubergines with a couple of pieces of kitchen paper on it

2. Heat a generous amount of light olive oil in a frying pan. When it is on the point of smoking, dip the slices of aubergine into the egg, then coat them in breadcrumbs and drop them into the frying pan

3. Allow them to brown on one side for about 1 minute then turn over and fry until both sides are brown

4. After about 6-7 slices, scrape out the pan and add a little more oil. Repeat until all the slices are fried. Serve immediately

Mamma always saved the leftover crusty baguettes or ciabatta from Saturday lunch so this dish featured as a regular Sunday dinner with some salad and cheese; we needed something light after the traditional English roast for lunch.

Arrosto di Vitello con Tartufo
Roast Veal with Truffle

Fillet of prime veal, slow roasted until it literally melts in the mouth, rich with truffle and buttery juices … need I say more! Veal is a lean, delicate and tender meat. Because it is lean it can easily become dry, so cooking it right – so that it falls apart in its own juices – is essential to the success of this dish. Unfortunately it can be quite hard to find in this country unless you go to a good butcher or the local farm shop. All the more incentive to leave the security of your local supermarket and head out to the green fields to find your food!

Truffles are seasonal but are increasingly available in delicatessens and some supermarkets throughout the year. They can be expensive but are worth every penny. Truffles and veal for the occasional Sunday roast are what good food and good eating are all about. If you cannot find any, use a few teaspoons of good quality truffle oil or, better still, buy some good quality truffle butter from an Italian delicatessen. This will usually have large chunks of truffle preserved in the butter (it is also great for stirring through *tagliolini*).

Another alternative to truffle that makes a delicious Italian-style roast is to wrap cloves of garlic in sage leaves and stuff them in the small holes.

200g pancetta	100g butter
1 small black truffle	Olive oil
800g veal fillet	250ml veal or beef stock

PREP:

1 Cube the pancetta and thinly slice the truffle

2 Season the meat well with salt and pepper

3 Make small slits all over the fillet with a sharp knife and insert a small cube of pancetta or a slice of truffle into each slit

4 Pre-heat the oven to 180°C

COOK:

1. Heat the butter and a few glugs of olive oil in a roasting dish until they begin to spit. Brown the fillet, then cover with well-buttered foil and a lid if possible

2. Transfer to the middle shelf of the oven for 50 minutes, turning from time to time and adding the prepared stock to keep the meat moist at all times

3. Once it is cooked keep the meat covered but allow it to rest for at least 10 minutes out of the oven

4. Cut into thick slices and serve with its own juices on warm plates

We would have this dish in the winter as it is really rich and warming. The arrosto would always be accompanied by mounds of "le patate della nonna", so named because my grandmother's potatoes were legendary. You can never cook too many roast potatoes when my family is around.

Pesce Spada al Burro e Limone
Panfried Swordfish Steaks

Swordfish is one of Italy's most popular fish. They are large so you are most likely to find them sold as steaks. The colour of the flesh varies according to their diet: some North American varieties are quite pink, Mediterranean varieties usually whiter.

The robust flesh has a remarkably delicate, fresh flavour rather like tuna and should be treated in much the same way as tuna, cooked to taste from medium rare to well done, although it can dry out a little if overcooked. The lemon penetrates the flesh and begins to cook the fish while it is marinating so it doesn't need long in the pan.

Keep things simple by serving it with a fresh green salad.

4 swordfish steaks	A handful of parsley
Salt and pepper	100g butter
2 lemons	1 small glass of fish stock (or white wine)
A drizzle of olive oil	

PREP:

1 Season the swordfish steaks with salt and pepper, squeeze the lemons over them with a drizzle of olive oil and let them marinate for about 20 minutes

2 Roughly chop the parsley

COOK:

1. Heat a generous knob of butter in a pan; add the marinated swordfish steaks with all the lemon juices

2. Cook on a medium heat, browning each side and watching the flesh turn whiter up the sides of the steaks until the lines meet, or to your specification, then set aside on a plate (warm if possible)

3. Turn up the heat under the pan, add fish stock or wine to deglaze, picking up all the juices and sediment from the bottom of the pan. Add the rest of the butter and the chopped parsley, and allow the liquid to reduce a little

4. Place the swordfish steaks on serving plates and pour the buttery juices over them. Serve immediately with a wedge of lemon

Merluzzo al Vermouth
Cod with Vermouth

This recipe typifies the way the Italians eat their fish – fresh and simply cooked. It sticks to the principles of minimal interference but maximum flavour. Dry vermouth brings out the meatiness of the cod and the lemon cuts through the sweetness of the almonds to create a well balanced dish. You could use any other heavy white fish: hoki and monkfish are both excellent. This is a good light dish for a summer evening or quick lunch. Serve it with a few boiled new potatoes, lightly poached fennel, or a salad.

Serves 4

4 cod fillets	A large glass of dry vermouth
A bunch of parsley	1 lemon
Olive oil	
A handful of almonds or pine nuts (optional)	

PREP:

1 Rinse the cod and chop the parsley

2 Preheat the oven to 180°C

COOK:

1. Put the fillets of cod in an overproof dish, brush them on both sides with olive oil, season well with salt and pepper, sprinkle over parsley and nuts. Pour on the vermouth and squeeze the lemon over them

2. Bake for 10-15 minutes until the fish has turned golden brown on top and flakes a little when you press it with the back of a fork. Serve with a wedge of lemon and a spoonful or two of the juices from the pan

Every Friday is still fish day in most Italian households so no recipe collection would be complete without it. This one is fresh and exceedingly simple, which is the way fish is best served.

Crema all'Amaretto
Amaretto Cream

Amaretto is my favourite liqueur. Something so sweet and rich yet lusciously aromatic has to be a winner in any dessert and this is no exception. It tastes as good as a *pannacotta* but without the cooking time. It can be made in advance and kept in the fridge for a day if covered. For a silky *crema* and to ensure that the *amaretto* infuses the cream it is vital that the biscuits are crushed to a fine powder. The coffee grinder attachment on most blenders guarantees this.

A sophisticated but utterly simple after-dinner treat, these look fantastic served in sexy little espresso cups with a tiny spoon and an amaretto biscuit on the side.

Makes 8	
100g *amaretti* biscuits	1 egg
4 tbsp strong espresso coffee	Generous splash of amaretto liqueur
350g mascarpone (or cream cheese)	Cocoa powder to decorate (optional)
40g sugar	

PREP:

1 Crush the *amaretti* biscuits to a powder

2 Make some strong *espresso* coffee

3 Combine the *amaretti* biscuits with the coffee and add the mascarpone, sugar, egg and *amaretto* liqueur

4 Whisk well to a smooth, pale, thick cream

5 Spoon into espresso cups or ramekins and refrigerate for at least 1 hour

6 Sprinkle with cocoa powder to serve

Torta di Mele
Apple Layer Cake

I have had long discussions as to whether *torta di mele* is apple cake or apple pie. I was recently told by a guest that it was the best apple pie he had ever had – so it doesn't really matter what you call it.

The cake mixture is more like soft dough than a traditional cake mix, and the lack of eggs would make most cake-makers nervous but I can assure you it works extremely well. It is layered and looks fabulous when sliced through: slivers of apples and raisins speckled with spices, sitting between layers of golden, crumbly cake.

If you don't have all three sugars, don't worry. I have made it with just white sugar and it is fine but

is no bite in the sauce. Basil in an apple sauce comes as a surprise to most people so I make them taste it before I tell them what it is. It's strange how people's preconceptions stop them trying new things. If I am feeling indulgent I love to serve it with a little double cream.

I like the way brown sugar melts and caramelises the fruit so well and using icing sugar means there

We had a huge Bramley apple tree in our garden that only just survived the 1987 storm and continues to provide box after box of ripe, tasty fruit every year. Dad would use the 'long arm' to cut the apples from the tree and would call as he snipped them so my brother and I could move in for the catch. I have had many a Bramley on the head and I can tell you that they hurt, or at least would have done had we not all been rolling around in fits of laughter. After the first harvest each year we would prepare this cake.

1. To make the pastry, put the flour in a bowl and make a well

2. Add the white sugar, baking powder, lemon zest, melted butter, cream and rum. Cream together into a thick dough and allow the mixture to rest for half an hour

3. In a separate bowl mix the chopped apples, raisins, nuts, brown sugar and cinnamon

4. Spoon half the cake mixture into the tin and press down with the back of your hand to make a thin, even, unbroken base. Follow with the apple filling and top with the rest of the cake mixture. You can do this by flattening out a handful of mix at a time in your palm then laying it over the fruit, making sure there are no gaps

5. Place in a pre-heated oven at 150°C for 30 minutes

6. Meanwhile, for the sauce, simply peel, core and chop an apple. Blend it in an electric blender with the basil, icing sugar and the juice of 1 lemon

7. Turn out the cake onto a serving plate and allow it to cool. Dust with icing sugar and serve with cold or warm apple sauce

For 8-12 slices

300g flour	225g butter
60g white sugar	80ml double cream
2 tsp baking powder	A small glass of rum or brandy (optional)
Zest of 1 lemon	
For the Filling:	**For the Sauce:**
4 Bramley apples	1 eating apple (e.g. Cox's)
50g raisins	5 basil leaves
50g walnuts	50g icing sugar
30g pine nuts	1 lemon
40g soft brown sugar	
2 tsp cinnamon	
Juice of 1 lemon	

PREP:

1 Melt the butter

2 Grate the zest of 1 lemon

3 Peel, core and thinly slice 4 Bramley apples. Squeeze over them the juice of 1 lemon to stop them going brown

4 Butter and flour a releasable cake tin (or greaseproof it)

5 Roughly chop the walnuts and pine nuts

6 Preheat the over to 150°C

A Persian Kitchen

Introduction to Persian Cuisine

With its subtle use of fresh and dried fruits, the delicate blend of aromatic herbs, a balanced choice and variety of ingredients as well as the rich colours and emphasis on aesthetics it is not surprising that Iran boasts one of the most sophisticated cuisines of Western Asia.

The cuisine described here as 'Persian' has a history that dates back to the sixth century BC, when Cyrus the Great, the leader of a tribe called the Pars, created an empire whose influence was felt in the whole of the ancient world from the valley of the Indus to Greece and Egypt. Their rich lands with the Caspian Sea to the north and the Persian Gulf to the south.

Persia was long considered the centre of civilisation of much of the ancient world. Time and energy were focused on the sciences, mathematics and the arts. Extensive irrigation systems watered the dry central plains by effectively tapping the icecaps of the surrounding mountains. Methods of preserving fresh foods, including drying in the sun were perfected, enabling the Persians to travel further than ever before. As they travelled and spread their knowledge they took various ingredients with them including the humble aubergine, dried fruits and nuts, and much-prized saffron.

The ancient Persians – like Iranians today – believed that dining should nourish the mind and spirit as well as the body. From extravagantly dressed belly dancers to simple prayers embroidered on tablecloths, meals are accompanied by some form of music, poetry and philosophy.

With their travels and conquests Persians spread their knowledge and understanding of ingredients, the importance of balance and beauty in cooking, and the socially significant role of dining. Lemons, pome-granates, peaches and pistachios reached the Mediterranean and were readily adopted by all who tasted them. They introduced new fruits, vegetables and herbs, and the use of flowers in cooking was certainly founded on the knowledge of Persian apothecaries and cooks.

While the Persians fought the Greeks, the Chinese were sending their first missions across land and sea to explore the West but their purpose was trade not conquest. Rice, which was to become the staple of Iran, arrived via the Silk Route and citrus fruits were taken back to China.

The Crusades brought Persian cuisine across Europe to England. Soldiers and knights brought back rare and delicate spices and herbs to give to their wives and lovers and thus created a demand that would, in time, fuel modern trade. Roses were a central element: apothecaries and the aristocracy demanded the delicate blossoms to flavour foods and scent the often fetid air. Many of the medieval recipes still familiar today that call for oranges and cinnamon, barberries and quinces are of Persian origin.

However, our experience of authentic Persian cuisine is limited. In this chapter I hope to right this wrong by explaining how to recreate this colourful, rich and exciting cuisine in your own home.

Flavours of a Persian Kitchen

Characterised by delicate flavourings and subtle aromas, Persian cuisine favours the use of flowers, fruit and herbs rather than heady spices. Fresh ingredients are abundant in season, and dried fruits, vegetables, pulses and nuts, from sweet cherries to peaches, peas to pistachios are ready for use out of season.

It was the use of flowers, such as the rose, in cooking that made Persian cuisine so elegantly distinct and sought after. The ancient Greek and Roman aristocracies were always in search of innovations that would set them apart from the masses; they found one in Persian saffron. These dried stigmas of the crocus flower became exceedingly popular because of their costly rarity and the difficulty of collecting them. The golden threads are picked from each flower by hand, with more than 75,000 flowers needed to produce just half a kilo of saffron. Saffron is still used today in most Persian recipes from fragrant rice dishes to intensely flavoured meat stews.

The expert blending of fruit and nuts is another striking facet of Persian cuisine. Pomegranate juice and seeds are used for colour and tartness, sour cherries for piquancy, dates for sweetness, walnuts for texture and richness.

Instead of stock or wine in stews lime or lemon juice, tamarind juice or unripe grape juice called *verjuice* were used to give a characteristic sour note to certain dishes. Yogurt and goats' cheese was widespread and is still used as a marinade to tenderise meats. Meals are often accompanied by a Yogurt dip or a herb-flavoured Yogurt drink called *doogh*.

Lamb is the favoured meat in Persian cuisine: young, sweet and tender. Kid is also used but is not always easy to find. Whole fish are served to honoured guests and are seen as a statement of wealth and generosity, perhaps because originally only a minority of people living near the coast had access to fresh fish. Chicken and beef are used but not as frequently. Seafood and pork are prohibited for Muslims although non-Muslim Iranians would include them in their diet.

One of Iran's most important exports is the exclusive black caviar from the sturgeon fish that is native to the Caspian Sea. It has become a billion-pound worldwide industry. For those unable to obtain or afford real caviar, 'poor man's caviar' is made from aubergines, another ubiquitous export. This vegetable – also known as the Iranian potato – is served daily in traditional Iranian homes in one form or another.

Persian cuisine is often confused with that of its Middle Eastern neighbours but what sets it apart is the abundant use of rice. Not any sort of rice but the high quality, unpolished, long grain rice known as *patna* rice. Other varieties available in Iran include *gilani, champa, rasmi, anbarbu, mowlai, sadri, khanjari, shekari and doodi*.

Wheat breads are secondary to rice. The flat bread *nane levash* is the most popular. Unlike bread, rice is not an accompaniment; it is the main dish of every meal at every table; all else is peripheral.

Contents of a Persian Store Cupboard

Rice – unpolished long grain
Dried Berries (Cranberries, Sultanas, etc.)
Pistachio nuts
Almonds
Angelica
Tea
Crystallised Sugar
Aubergines
Mung Beans
Chick Peas

Dried Fruits (Apricots, Limes, Peaches, etc.)
Dried Orange and Lemon Peel
Vegetable and Seed Oils
Clarified Butter and Rendered Fats
Yogurt
Radish
Walnuts
Tomato Paste
Pomegranate and Pomegranate Paste
Rose Petals and Rose Water
Lemons
Mint

Saffron
Cumin
Caraway Seeds
Turmeric
Cinnamon
Black Pepper
Nutmeg
Nigella Seeds
Persian Basil
Garlic Chives
Marjoram
Watercress
Tarragon
Fenugreek
Bay Leaves
Spinach
Parsley
Dill

Lessons learnt along the way...

The familiar adage 'you are what you eat' is an ancient Iranian belief. 'Diet', in its original definition, was a way of weakening or strengthening human character. Heat and temper could be alleviated and balanced by the consumption of cold foods. Sickness and coolness (i.e. depression) could be alleviated by eating 'hot' foods. Zoroaster, the founder of the ancient dualistic religion of Persia, first promoted this ideology sometime in the eighth or seventh century BC. It was reinforced later by Hippocrates, who developed theories of the hot-cold balance of 'humours' in the body, similar to *yin* and *yang* in the East.

'Hot' and 'cold' food has nothing to do with temperature. Children who are seen as hyperactive and aggressive are often fed 'cold' foods to calm them down while sickly, docile children are given 'hot' foods to wake them up and give them a spring in their step. 'Hot' foods are usually rich in calories and carbohydrates such as wheat, animal fat, and sugar. 'Cold' foods are lighter and perhaps dairy based; they include fish, fresh vegetables, fruit and Yogurt. The choice of hot or cold food was said to reflect character: It is easy to see why you might be considered delicate and noble if you ate fruit and food flavoured with roses and jasmine but harsh and selfish if you ate large amounts of red meat.

When planning meals, cooks take account of people's nature and state of health, and of the season, striving to balance meals on the basis of these elements. In the summer, for example, bread, cheese and Yogurt, followed by fruit, would constitute a normal meal. In the winter, stews and soups containing dumplings and meat are more common. Each individual dish must also be balanced: for example, walnuts are a 'hot' food and are usually used in dishes that include pomegranate, a 'cold' food. Perhaps because it is very important to

serve an abundance of food and meat is expensive, protein is often found from other sources. Legumes and pulses such as mung beans, fava beans, chick peas and lentils are consumed almost daily in Iranian households: they are toasted and salted and offered as appetisers and nibbles; or added to stews and rice dishes. Nuts are also a good source of protein and healthy oils and are used in many dishes and as appetisers and garnishes.

You will never be really hungry if you visit an Iranian home. Apart from the feasts for breakfast, lunch and dinner, there are always bowls of fresh and dried fruit, nuts and snacks tn hand, and the frequent drinking of sweet teas staves off any major cravings.

When I was younger and came home from school, my grandmother would always have peeled a pomegranate, taken out all the little juicy red bits and put them in a bowl for us to pick at. Mum said that in Iran that is what you would be able to pick up at fruit stalls on the way home so to my gran this was the equivalent of a chocolate bar.

Good health and godliness are believed to go hand in hand. As a result a guest is seen as a gift from God. You should always be ready to welcome friends and strangers with food and drink. Tourists travelling to the Middle East are often overwhelmed by offerings of tea and sweets in every shop and have touching stories of being invited to poor homes and being offered what seems to be the hosts' last morsel of food. Because of this Iranians always try to cook more food than their guests could possibly eat:

"The amount of food you serve represents how much you value your guests. The table had to be covered

with food. You can't make this food for one person or two. It seems ridiculous to us. Even now I have that habit. When I look at cookbooks and they say 'serves four' I think that it's ridiculous and always double up on the quantities. I can't do otherwise; I'm too worried there won't be enough for everyone. Where other people offered tea and biscuits, mum would have masses of platters of fruit, nuts, rice and salads.

Traditionally a white cloth called a *sofreh*, often embroidered with traditional prayers or poetry is laid out over a Persian rug or table. There are no formal table settings because you never know how many people might walk through the door. The main dishes are surrounded by a number of accompaniments from pickles to Yogurt dips, condiments and breads. The aim is to completely cover every bit of the white tablecloth with delicious colourful foods.

Leftovers are common, but many of the dishes taste better re-heated as the flavours have time to develop.

The principles of aesthetics ensure that the diet is varied and colourful, its tastes exotic. Yet it is essentially a simple cuisine. Persian food is extremely healthy, depending of course on the amount you eat, something harder to control than you might imagine:

If you go to people's houses and finish what is on your plate they will inevitably serve you more. By the time you respond to their question you already have another serving so you learn to just accept it. They always want you to eat more. If you don't you run the risk of offending them.

Manners are very important to Iranians. For traditional families this means removing their shoes before entering the dining room. This is because they used to eat on rugs on the floor rather than at a table. Some still do. When everyone is sitting down the platters are brought out, which usually takes no time at all:

To dive in to the food as if it were your last meal would be insulting to your hostess. Being the first to dip in is difficult so they are usually quick to invite their guests to eat.

Although there is no fixed structure for a meal there are certain *mokhalafat* (accompaniments) that are almost always served. To begin you might be offered *sabzi*: a platter of fresh herbs such as basil, coriander, tarragon, watercress and mint, along with lettuce and radishes. These would come with breads in which to wrap them. Persian pickles and relishes are also considered essential on most dinner tables, replacing salt and pepper. Fresh tomato, sliced cucumber and green onion as well as lemon juice and Yogurt accompany every meal to cleanse and refresh the palate; green onion as it is apparently inoffensive in smell and taste compared to red or white onion; cinnamon, cloves, and cardamom are also commonly used to gently relieve any unpleasant after-effects of over-indulgent dining. They are chewed to cleanse the breath and aid digestion.

When the main meal has been cleared away, those sitting round the table begin to peel fruit, filling more platters and putting them on the table for everyone to share. Rice pudding, ice cream or sweet pastries may be served to conclude the meal.

For desserts there are basically two that matter: 'baghlava' — more syrupy than sugary and really not so sweet, and saffron rice pudding, again not rich and creamy like English rice pudding but light and fresh.

Tea is as much of a social prop in Iranian culture as it is in British or Chinese culture: it is drunk to start the day, welcome guests, break working hours, and is served at social and business events. Meals are always accompanied by endless supplies of *cha-I*, sweet black tea served in a glass with a silver handle from a samovar, a pot on a stand with a candle in it to keep the tea warm:

To sweeten the tea you put a sugar cube in your mouth and drink the tea through it. So bad for your teeth! There are some cubes that are more like boiled sweets: they don't dissolve as quickly and last for a whole cup.

Tisanes from Iran are used for medicinal purposes all over the world: chamomile aids relaxation and promotes sleep; jasmine is an anti-inflammatory and mood enhancer. Flower tisanes such as rose, jasmine and violet are as popular as herbal tisanes made from ginger, saffron, fennel and anise.

Coffee is the third most common drink for Iranians. For the purist, coffee beans are roasted and crushed immediately before brewing. Coffee is offered three times after a guest's arrival, usually in very small cups without handles. To refuse coffee would be deemed an insult in a traditional household, sipping it loudly a compliment.

As with most nationalities, food is used in celebration. *Shab-e yaldâ* or Yuletide is celebrated in December with friends and family calling on each other throughout the night, bringing a mixture of seven (a sacred number) dried fruits and nuts called *âjeel*. *Nowruz*, a rebirth festival that is the equivalent of New Year and the most important holiday of the year, is celebrated on the first day of spring. The table is set with seven traditional dishes and other symbolic items such as eggs for fertility, and wheat and lentils for abundance.

Such annual celebrations are marked with special feasts but every meal time is an opportunity for music, poetry, literature and dance providing enjoyment for both body and mind. When Iranians dine in restaurants they do not behave in the same way as Europeans:

We don't sit round a table and have a normal dinner, sipping a glass of wine over a meal. It's more about having a party, singing and dancing; and it's loud. People don't come in couples; they turn up with five or fifteen friends. There is always a big stage area and inevitably at some point during the evening a belly dancer appears. You drink tea all through the meal and sing. ... Immediately after the main course there is no 'shall we have a coffee or dessert'; it's straight onto the dance floor. Basically if you go to someone's house it's all about eating but if you go to a restaurant it's all about entertainment.

The best foods are found in people's homes and the best recipes are those passed from mother to daughter. All the more reason for you to try these recipes and create a Persian feast for friends and family.

Ash-e Torcht
Dried Fruit Soup

Chelow
Saffron Rice with Yogurt and Lemon

Morasa Polow
Jewelled Rice

Maahi Kabab
Lemon Saffron Grilled Fish

Khoresht-e Bâdenjân
Aubergine Stew

Recipes

Morgh
Fragrant Roast Chicken

Sardast-e Barreh Tu Por
Aromatic Stuffed Saddle of Lamb

Khoresht-e Fesenjân
Duck Stew with Walnuts and Pomegranate

Koofteh
Treasure Meat Dumplings

Dolmeh-ye Barg-e Mo
Stuffed Vine Leaves

Baghlava
Fragrant Honey and Nut Filo Pastries

Ash-e Torcht [Dried Fruit Soup]

Ash-e Torcht
Dried Fruit Soup

This traditional starter is enjoyed by family and friends all year round. It's a fabulous introduction to the use of fruit in savoury dishes, balancing the sweetness of the fruits with the freshness of the herbs. There are very few Persian vegetarian dishes and this soup is typically served with meatballs but you could omit them and add the seasonings directly to the rice broth.

100g walnuts	100g long grain rice
75g dried apricots	Pinch of salt
75g dried prunes	50g sugar
2 onions	50ml white wine vinegar
1 tbsp ground cinnamon	50g parsley
200g minced beef	1 tbsp butter
5 or 6 mint leaves	
1 litre of vegetable stock (or water and 1 vegetable stock cube)	

PREP:

1 Chop walnuts, dried apricots and prunes

2 Grate one onion and chop the other

3 In a bowl mix minced beef, half the cinnamon powder, the grated onion, salt, and finely chopped mint

4 Make meatballs by taking a walnut-sized piece of seasoned mince, wet your hands, and roll the meat in your palms to create balls

COOK:

1. In a large pot bring a litre of stock or water and a vegetable stock cube to the boil

2. Add a pinch of salt and the rice. Bring it back to the boil and simmer for 15 minutes

3 In a frying pan sauté the chopped onion in butter

4. Add the chopped prunes to the rice pot and simmer for a further 10 minutes

5. Add meatballs, apricots, walnuts and fried onions to the rice pot and simmer for a further 15 minutes

6. Add sugar, vinegar and finely chopped parsley. Simmer for another 10 minutes

7. Season and add another touch of cinnamon. Serve immediately

Chelow
Saffron Rice with Yogurt and Lemon

Rice is eaten every day and served with almost every meal so this classic dish is a regular on the Iranian dinner table. It is simple and satisfying.

There are several types of rice available to us and suitable for this dish: unpolished long grain rice is the best, followed by basmati, with American standard long grain in third place. Iranians usually soak their rice according to its age and cook it for a very short time. As we are unlikely to know the age of our rice it is just as effective to soak it to break down some of the starches and cook it as usual, aiming for a light fluffy grain. *Chelow* is delicately flavoured with bright strands of saffron and cooked with yogurt and lemon juice to prevent the grains from breaking and to make it whiter. The rice forms a beautiful golden brown skin on the bottom of the pan that cooks until it is crisp. It is called the *tahdeeg*.

I guess for me rice was like chips. It is especially popular with children developing their tastes and for those not up to trying so many new things.

The way your tahdeeg turns out defines the calibre of cook you are; the crunchier your crust the better!

500g long grain rice	2 tbsp Yogurt
2 tbsp salt	1 tsp lemon juice
2 litres of water	1 egg
Small pinch of saffron filaments	100ml vegetable or seed oil
Pinch of sugar	25g butter

PREP:

1 Wash rice several times, soak for at least half an hour and no more than 2 hours in well salted water. Rinse when ready to use

2 In a pestle and mortar grind saffron stems with sugar, mix with 4 tbsp of warm water and allow to infuse

COOK:

1. Bring 2 litres of salted water to the boil

2. Rinse the rice, pour it into the salted water and bring back to a rolling boil

3. Add a tablespoon of yogurt and lemon juice to the water and stir

4. Turn down the heat and simmer for 10-15 minutes, testing to see when it is ready. The time will vary according to the type of rice and the thickness of the pot

5. Once cooked, rinse the rice with tepid water so that it does not continue to cook. Fluff and separate the grains with a fork. Set aside

6. In a bowl, whisk the egg with half the saffron water and the other tablespoon of yogurt; add a spoonful of rice, stir and fluff so the grains separate

7. Pour a little oil into a non-stick pan over a moderate heat

8. Sprinkle the eggy saffron rice mix into the hot oil. Do not stir

9. Build up a layer of yellow rice then continue to sprinkle the rest of the rice over it, building layer after layer, ensuring that the grains are separated as they are forked in

10. With the handle of a wooden spoon or a chopstick make a couple of holes through the rice to the bottom of the pan to allow the steam to escape

11. Cover well, creating a seal. Steam for 30 minutes on a low heat so the *tahdeeg* base doesn't burn

12. When ready dip the base of the saucepan into a bowl/sink of cold water to loosen the bottom of the *tahdeeg*

13. Spoon off a little of the rice and mix it with the remaining saffron water as a garnish

14. Turn out the remaining rice. It should stay together with a crisp *tahdeeg* skin on the top. Pour a little melted butter over it to make it shine

Morasa Polow
Jewelled Rice

This dish has transcended time and holds pride of place on the tables of many nations. In India it is *pullao* with brightly coloured dyed grains of rice added to white rice; in the Caribbean *pelaf* with peas and carrots added for colour. Turkish *pilav* and Russian *plov* have their own variations but all descend from the Persian dish. The original is usually the best and this is no exception. For Iranians *morasa polow* encapsulates the lightness and delicacy of flavourings, an aesthetically pleasing colour palate, and a generous giving of fortune in the form of rice – symbol of abundance and fertility.

Pinch of saffron stems	1 tbsp ground cinnamon
500g basmati rice	4 cloves
Large pinch of salt	30g toasted pistachios
4 cardamom pods	30g toasted almonds
1 orange	450ml chicken stock
50ml light seed oil or vegetable oil	3 tbsp sugar
	50ml water
50g barberries or dried cranberries	

PREP:

1 Soak the saffron in about 4 tsp of warm water

2 Wash the rice in a colander under running water

3 Crush the cardamom pods and extract the seeds

4 Peel the orange with a vegetable peeler and cut the rind into fine strips eliminating as much pith as possible

COOK:

1. Heat the oil in a heavy-based pot

2. Fry the cranberries or barberries for 1 minute, drain and set aside. Using the same oil fry the cinnamon, turmeric and cardamom seeds for 1 minute

3. Put back the dried fruit and add the rice and cloves to the cooking pot. Stir to coat the rice with the spices

4. Add the stock and bring to the boil, then cover and simmer for 30 minutes. Lift the lid half way through cooking and check to see that the rice is steaming and the water has been absorbed

5. Put the sugar, orange peel and water in a separate pan and simmer for 10 minutes to create a caramel. Add the pistachio nuts and stir to coat them completely

6. Once the rice is cooked, fluff with a fork and stir in the caramelised nuts

7. Serve garnished with toasted almonds

Maahi Kabab
Lemon Saffron Grilled Fish

Putting a whole fish on the table is the customary way of displaying your wealth and demonstrating your generosity to your guests so this is a must at large gatherings and celebrations. Most fish can be used for this recipe but a white, fleshy fish lends itself well to the fresh herbs. The herbs are finely chopped in what the French call a *chiffonnade*: simply roll them together in a tight bundle and, using a sharp knife, finely chop them all together into long, thin strips, like delicate ribbons of chiffon.

50g coriander	1 whole fish (sea bass, sea bream, grouper, mahi mahi)
50g mint	
50g chervil (or parsley)	$^1/_2$ tsp saffron
2 fresh limes	Salt to taste
100ml extra virgin olive oil	

PREP:

1 Finely chop the herbs, keeping a few aside for the garnish

2 Add the olive oil and saffron, then the juice of two limes and a pinch of salt. Stir together to make a sauce

3 Clean and gut the fish, slitting it open from head to tail. Remove the fins but leave the head on. Wash and dry thoroughly

4 Rub sea salt inside and out

COOK:

1. Grill the fish at a high temperature for 5-10 minutes on each side until the skin crisps up

2. Lay a large sheet of aluminium foil on a baking tray, brush it in the middle with a little of the olive oil/ herb mix and place the fish on top

3. Brush the fish all over with the herb oil and fill the cavity with any that remains

4. Create a parcel by wrapping the edges of the foil together and twisting to create a seal

5. Cook in a medium oven for approximately 35 minutes, depending on the size of the fish

6. When cooked, serve whole on a platter with some thinly sliced fresh lemon and some green herbs

I always remember a huge fish on the table, decorated with slivers of lemon or carrot to look like scales; people didn't talk about the fact that it symbolised money, but everyone knew it.

Khoresht-e Bâdenjân
Aubergine Stew

Aubergine, the potato of Iran, is used in many dishes and is a very versatile vegetable. Like the potato it takes on different qualities when baked, fried, grilled or stewed. One really simple way to prepare it is to roast it with yogurt and cumin seeds, then add it to rice. Another popular way to serve it is in a thick stew known as a *koresht*. This really brings out the flavours and colours of this humble vegetable. Salting the sliced aubergine before cooking it removes the excess moisture and bitter juices, making it succulent and sweet. Like most Persian foods, the slower the stew is cooked the more fragrant and delicious it becomes. This is a particularly wonderful and warming dish on a cold winter's evening.

4 aubergines	1 tsp fenugreek seeds
800gm leg of lamb (boned)	3 tbsp tomato purée
2 onions	3 fresh tomatoes
Olive oil	1 lemon (juice only)
1 tsp turmeric	1 litre lamb stock

PREP:

1 Peel the aubergines, spread on a cloth and salt liberally. Leave for 20 minutes, then wipe dry

2 Trim lamb of excess fat

3 Slice onions. Skin and chop tomatoes

COOK:

1. Fry the aubergine in generous amounts of oil until the flesh has softened and caramelised

2. Meanwhile, in a frying pan heat a tablespoon of oil and add the fenugreek seeds. Fry until they pop, then add the onions and caramelise

3. Add turmeric and brown the meat

4. Add fresh tomatoes, tomato purée, and lemon juice

5. Add stock and bring to the boil

6. Cover and simmer for 1 hour 30 minutes

7. Add the aubergines and continue to simmer for another 30 minutes or until the meat is tender and the sauce has thickened

8. Serve with rice (of course)

Morgh
Fragrant Roast Chicken

This is a delicious meat 'rub' that can be used on a whole chicken or turkey or when roasting the breasts. It is the simplest of these recipes and probably the most modern. A wonderful Persian alternative to a Sunday roast using many of the flavours that we associate with Christmas: cranberries, cinnamon, oranges and lemons.

1 medium organic chicken	Salt
2 lemons	6 cloves
1 orange	80g dried cranberries
1/2 tsp cinnamon	1 tsp finely chopped fresh ginger
2 tbsp vinegar	2 tbsp honey
1/2 tsp pepper	2 tbsp oil
1/2 tsp ground fennel	
1/2 tsp freshly grated nutmeg	

PREP:

1 Pre-heat oven to 180°C

2 Wash and dry the chicken inside and out

3 Grate zest off lemon and orange, and quarter the fruit

4 In a pestle and mortar pound the cinnamon, pepper, fennel, nutmeg, cloves, two-thirds of the cranberries, and the ginger, with the lemon and orange zest, the juice of 1/2 lemon, and vinegar to create a paste

5 Mix the fragrant paste with honey

COOK:

1. Place the chicken in a lightly oiled roasting tin

2. Brush inside and out with fragrant paste and stuff the orange and lemon segments and the remaining cranberries into the cavity

3. Cover with foil and roast for 40 minutes, basting regularly with the juices. Remove the foil and roast for a further 15 minutes to allow the skin to brown and crisp up

4. Check the chicken is cooked by putting a skewer through the thick part of the thigh to check that the juices run clear. Serve with *chelow* or *polow*

Sardast-e Barreh Tu Por
Aromatic Stuffed Saddle of Lamb

Whole lambs are usually stuffed and roasted over a charcoal fire but as I imagine you won't be catering for a wedding party, the saddle is a wonderfully rich cut, perfectly shaped and marbled with fat for this dish. The saffron dyes the meat and gives it a comforting warm amber glow. It works well in both summer and winter as the fruit and nuts are deliciously indulgent but the combination is not heavy.

1kg saddle of lamb (boned)	50g almonds
Salt	50g sultanas
1/2 tsp cinnamon	50g sour cherries (optional)
80g basmati or long grain rice	1 lemon
1 onion	100g butter
50g apricots	1 tbsp saffron

PREP:

1 Wash and boil the rice in salted water for 20 minutes. Drain
2 Chop all the dried fruit and almonds into small pieces
3 Chop the onion
4 Unroll, clean and season the saddle
5 Steep saffron in 2 tbsp of water

COOK:

1. Fry the onion until it is soft, add the remaining dry stuffing ingredients and the rice. Set aside to cool

2. Spread out the lamb saddle, stuff with the rice mixture, then roll up tightly

3. Tie together with string, or skewer the edges together with toothpicks to secure

4. Brush the lamb all over with saffron liquid then smear over the butter, covering it completely

5. Cover with foil and roast in a medium over for 1 hour 20 minutes

6. Remove the foil, baste and continue to cook for a further 15-20 minutes

7. Allow the meat to rest, covered in foil, for at least 10 minutes before slicing and serving

Khoresht-e Fesenjân
Duck Stew with Walnuts and Pomegranate

Walnuts and pomegranate are the archetypal Persian ingredients; the walnuts give depth, flavour and texture that would not be so evident if it were not for the piquancy of the pomegranate. Traditionally this dish is made with the addition of meatballs but I prefer the taste of the dark duck meat alone in its powerful sauce. I take the skin off the duck after the initial browning. The fat is essential to enhance the flavour but the stew becomes too oily if it is left on throughout.

You can, of course, use other game birds such as pheasant or partridge when in season; even chicken cooked in the same way works well.

1 large jointed duck (or pheasant or chicken)	250g walnuts
A few glugs of olive oil for browning	1litre of pomegranate juice
	1 lemon
500ml chicken stock	1 pomegranate
1 small onion	Salt and sugar (to taste)

PREP:

1 Crush the walnuts in a pestle and mortar or blend roughly in a blender

2 Chop the onion

3 Cut the pomegranate in half, or peel it, and pop out all the red seed pods into a bowl catching all the juices

COOK:

1. Reduce the pomegranate juice in a pan with the juice of 1 lemon to one third of the original volume

2. Heat three glugs of oil in a pot, fry the crushed walnuts for 15 minutes over a low heat

3. Drain with a perforated spoon and add the duck to the pot. Brown all over

4 Remove duck, discard the fatty skin and set meat aside

5. Fry the onion in the remaining duck fat and oil until caramelised then return the skinned duck to the pot

6. Add stock, cover and simmer for 20 minutes

7. Add the reduced pomegranate juice, seasoning with salt and a pinch of sugar to taste and simmer uncovered for another 20 minutes to reduce the sauce to a thick consistency

8. Stir in the pomegranate pods and juices and let the meat rest for about 5 mins before serving with rice

Koofteh [Treasure Meat Dumplings]

Koofteh
Treasure Meat Dumplings

Meatballs in Iranian cuisine are not meatballs as we know them in the West. In some towns and villages there is still competition amongst cooks over who can make the biggest and the best.

Thanks to the joys of the food processor these balls of rice, herbs and meat filled with delicious 'treasures' can now be whipped up in no time, although I do still enjoy getting my hands in the bowl and pounding the meat as so that I can feel the consistency for myself and know if it needs more egg to moisten it. Rather than compete over size I prefer to make a batch of smaller meatballs with different fillings – walnuts and prunes, apricots and pistachios, hard-boiled quails' eggs with caramelised onions – to give a variety of flavour combinations.

Makes 12

150g rice	1 litre of lamb or veal stock
180g split peas	Turmeric
1kg minced beef, lamb or veal	
A handful of dill	Treasures:
A handful of parsley	50g apricots
4 sprigs of tarragon	50g pistachios
2 eggs	50g prunes
2 tbsp tomato purée	50g walnuts
Salt and pepper	1 onion
Olive oil	6 quails' eggs

PREP:

1 Chop the tarragon, parsley and dill

2 Chop pistachio and apricots together, and prunes and walnuts together

3 Hard boil and peel the quails' eggs

4 Boil the rice and split peas in separate pans of salted water for 20 minutes or until they soften

5 Fry the onion in a good glug of olive oil

COOK:

1. If you have a food processor with a dough blade use it to mix together meat, rice, tomato purée, whole eggs and fresh herbs. Season well with salt and pepper and turn out into a bowl. The mixture should hold together and be slightly tacky

2. Wet your hands and pinch off a satsuma-sized piece of meat mix. Roll it in your hand and make a dent in it with your thumb; spoon in a teaspoon of filling: some onion and a quail's egg; or apricot and pistachio; or prune and walnut. Draw the meat around the filling ensuring that it is completely sealed so the fillings won't escape. You might need a little more meat mix to seal it all up. Lay the meatballs on a cool surface or floured plate while you make the rest

3. In a large pan bring the stock to the boil and season with a little turmeric. Drop in the meatballs and cook on a low temperature for 25 minutes

4. Serve with salads and rice, or as a soup along with the broth in which they have been cooked

This of course required serious stamina and strength from the women who pounded the mixture by hand for hours until their arms ached and their backs hurt, all to ensure that the meatballs would not fall apart in the broth.

Dolmeh-ye Barg-e Mo [Stuffed Vine Leaves]

Dolmeh-ye Barg-e Mo
Stuffed Vine Leaves

Every Iranian cook has a special stuffing recipe for *dolmeh* that they will call on weekly if not daily. The balance of ingredients reflects the Persian eating ethos that 'hot' and 'cold' elements must be balanced – the rice with vegetables, the spice with herbs. The beauty of this stuffing is that it is just as delicious in aubergines, courgettes, peppers, tomatoes, and mushrooms, or wrapped in blanched cabbage leaves. Omit the meat to create a simple but delicious vegetarian filling.

Dolmeh make great snacks and as they have their own wrapper are perfect lunchbox or picnic foods to be enjoyed on a summer's day. Although served cold they are best not refrigerated. Before I made these I had been put off *dolmeh* and their Greek counterpart *dolmades* by those found in high street shops and even health food shops that are so variable in quality, texture and taste. They are usually stored too cold and many people eat them straight from the fridge and are therefore unable to taste the delicate herbs. The easiest way to decide how best to serve any cuisine is to think about where it comes from, the climate and typical dining style. In this way you'll never go far wrong.

30 vine leaves (or blanched cabbage leaves)	20g marjoram (small bunch)
1 medium onion	20g dill (small bunch)
90g long grain or basmati rice	1 tsp cinnamon
250g lamb, beef or veal	4-5 cloves
100g parsley	½ nutmeg, freshly grated
20g tarragon (small bunch)	1 tsp ground ginger
	Pinch of turmeric
	Salt and pepper

PREP:

1 If using fresh vine leaves or cabbage leaves, blanch for a couple of minutes in water with a squeeze of lemon juice in it

2 Finely chop the onion

3 Chop the fresh herbs

COOK:

1. Heat a generous glug of olive oil in a pan; add cinnamon and ground ginger, and heat until aromatic

2. Add the onion and caramelise, then add the meat and brown gently. Allow to cool

3. Meanwhile parboil the rice in water with a sprinkle of turmeric, cloves, and a pinch of salt

4 In a bowl mix the cooled meat, chopped herbs and rice. Add a generous amount of freshly grated nutmeg. Taste and adjust seasoning

5. Take one leaf and spoon one or two teaspoons of mixture into the centre, fold the bottom tightly up and over the stuffing, then the sides, finally folding over the top of the leaf and rolling it so the sealed edge is on the bottom. Set aside about three vine leaves

6. Pour some oil into a large pot and cover the bottom with the spare vine leaves

7. Arrange the prepared *dolmehs* in the pan, put a plate on top to weigh them down and cover with water

8. Cook gently for 1 hour, adding water if necessary

9. Serve with yogurt dips or a squeeze of lemon

Baghlava [Fragrant Honey and Nut Filo Pastries]

Baghlava
Fragrant Honey and Nut Filo Pastries

When the plentiful main courses have been served there is often little room for dessert so Iranians cover the table with fruit, drink litres of sweet black tea, chat, dance, and pick at small diamonds of *baghlava* and other sweets. Honey and cinnamon are famed for their medicinal properties in Iranian, Ayurvedic and oriental medicine, effective for all kinds of ailments from reducing cholesterol to relieving arthritis. Focus on that rather than the calories in each diamond and you'll enjoy them much more. Unless you are a pastry cook I would recommend buying filo pastry. It makes this dish a pleasure and so easy to prepare.

200g pistachios	1 packet of filo pastry
200g almonds	200ml clarified butter
A handful of green cardamom pods	100ml honey
1 tbsp cinnamon	4 tbsp water
150g sugar	4 tbsp rosewater

PREP:

1 In a blender place nuts and sugar and blitz until they are roughly chopped, leaving a handful behind for garnish

2 Crush the cardamom pods and throw away the husks

3 Melt butter and set aside

4 Melt honey and mix with water and rosewater

5 Butter and flour a square baking dish

COOK:

1. In a clean dry pan, toast the nuts with the cinnamon and cardamom. Allow to cool

2. Lay out the filo pastry and cut to the size of your tin. Brush one sheet with clarified butter, put in the tin, sprinkle over the nut mixture. Repeat with two layers of pastry, buttering each layer, then a layer of nuts, then pastry again until all the sheets have been used up. Set aside a few nuts

3. Brush with butter and cut a diamond pattern on top

4. Bake in a pre-heated oven at 200°C for 15-20 minutes, until the top layer is golden

5. While it is still warm, pour over the rose honey syrup, garnish with chopped pistachios and almonds, and slice diagonally through the pastry to create diamonds

TIP:
To cut the sweetness and as an aid to digestion you could serve the baghlava with a pot of fresh mint tea. Rather than tea bags simply boil a pan of water and throw in a bunch of fresh mint, allow it to infuse for about 8 minutes and pour.

Persian desserts are more syrupy and sticky than sweet, much lighter than you would expect. We graze on them after a meal in between dancing and chatting.

A Caribbean Kitchen

Introduction to Caribbean Cuisine

The beautiful, bounteous island of St. Vincent was the home of my friend Sonia's mother and thus the focus of this chapter. Although elements of its cuisine are unique it shares the ingredients, dishes and culinary styles of its neighbours.

The original people of the Caribbean islands, the Ciboney, migrated from northern South America. They were superseded by the Arawak, fishermen and faming people who in turn succumbed to the warrior Caribs. The indigenous people of St. Vincent had a primitive, but essential knowledge and understanding of the fruits and vegetables, fish and mammals they could eat, a knowledge that would eventually help sustain the lives of those who came to take the islands from them and who introduced crops of a completely different nature.

Little remains of the early indigenous cuisine except a few ingredients. The Arawaks grew roots like cassava, from which they made a fine flour *farine* to bake bread; they cultivated sweet potatoes and arrowroot to provide a digestible nutritive starch to supplement their diet of fish and meats. They had the earliest 'cook-up' also known as 'boileen' or 'pepper pot', which would be kept boiling constantly over a central fire. Into this the villagers added whatever animal they had caught or vegetables they had grown, topping it up with water to create a stew that would serve as breakfast, lunch and dinner. The Caribbean cuisine we recognise today has grown and developed from the influences of the four main ethnic groups who came to dominate the lands: European, African, American and Indian.

Like most of its Caribbean neighbours, St. Vincent was first settled by Europeans looking to expand their empire and exploit the lands. The Spanish brought cattle, chickens, goats, sheep, horses, and donkeys that changed both the diet and way of life in the Caribbean. British colonialists later contributed produce such as onions, garlic and wheat, and certain dishes such as roast beef, yeast-risen bread and fruit cakes that are still popular today. They also brought items that are today more synonymous with the islands than their 'homeland' such as breadfruits – once a staple for slaves – limes and mangos. The colonial settlers planted bananas, plantains, coffee, coconuts and oranges, and one crop that was so successful that it became the mainstay of the land: sugar cane. All these crops, but especially sugar, were labour intensive. The indigenous people were fiercely rebellious and did not take well to the enforced hard labour and harsh treatment from the invaders. Working conditions were so poor, the hours so long and the work so arduous that the indigenous population was largely wiped out. This led to the search for alternative labour and the massive importation of African slaves in the seventeenth century.

African slaves from different tribes brought with them many styles of cooking and new crops such as *okra*, *calalloo* (a green, leafy, spinach-like vegetable), *ackee*

(a fruit that looks like a peach), and various varieties of yams. To improve the bland diet they were given, slaves used what spices and peppers they could grow on the small dry plots assigned to them: chilli peppers, bay leaves, chives and ginger survived the extremes and pepped up almost every basic food.

The slaves were usually denied fresh meat or fish and so developed ways to preserve it such as salting and sun-drying. They brought their own traditions too: jerk pork, for example, was introduced by the Cormantee slaves from West Africa. Traditionally, these men were hunters who at home would roast the pigs they caught over hot coals and season them heavily with spices to preserve them for the long trek back to their settlements. The 'jerking' process of preservation is one that has grown in popularity and diversity in other nations such as South Africa, Australia and the USA.

Because of the proximity to South America there was inevitable trade and transactions bringing beans, corn, various types of peppers and potatoes. These ingredients supplemented the poor diet with essential protein and vitamins, and were all hardy plants suitable for growing on spare farmland and in backyards. In later history, Indian indentured workers brought an ingredient that had a dramatic and lasting effect on the nation's cuisine: curry. Dishes such as *pelau*, curry, *roti* and *dhal* were greedily adopted.

Women were the cooks in most households from plantation owner to workhouse. They would take the new ingredients and prepare them in a way they were familiar with, perhaps trying old recipes with new foods and on occasion new recipes with old foods. As the peoples mixed and intermarried they became known as *creole* and so too did their food. Five centuries have shaped a unique character and cuisine.

The flavours of a Caribbean Kitchen

Like the traditional stew that comes out of the *pepper pot*, the flavours of Caribbean cuisine have developed over time. Imported ingredients mixed well with the fruits of the land and the vibrant tropical sea. Goat and lamb found their place alongside conch, shrimp and lobster.

The Caribbean flavour is based on hot chilli peppers, fresh fruit and spices. Although the food is predominantly hot, a careful palate recognises a more subtle layer of sweet fruits, nuts, herbs and rum, the elixir of life so frequently used. One ingredient that features prominently in savoury and sweet dishes is the Caribbean or Jamaican pimento known as *allspice*, thus named because once crushed the berry tastes like a mixture of nutmeg, cloves, cinnamon and pepper.

Most people in St. Vincent grow herbs and spices to provide fresh ingredients: chilli peppers, thyme, chives (pronounced sives), and watercress grow in the most basic gardens. Lucky ones have mango and papaya trees.

Ginger, native to Jamaica, is far more pungent than its Chinese relative. The fiery creamy flesh is first grated then mixed with sugar and made into one of the most popular Caribbean drinks: ginger beer. Despite the abundance of fresh produce in these fertile, sunny islands, many people, from slaves to indentured workers, were denied access or the tools to produce enough food to sustain themselves, so they learned to preserve what they could. Over time, Caribbean people mastered the art of pickling and preserving. Using what spices they could and the readily available sugar, they made jams, marmalades, jellies, sauces and pickles to suit every palate and dish. The most popular lime and mango pickles, known as *kuchela*, undoubtedly descend from Indian style chutneys.

When my mother came to England in 1968 she wasn't able to recreate the island flavours. Ingredients were sparse and she survived on custard, the only thing she could stomach in the canteen at the nurses' college where she was studying. She told me the scrambled eggs were grey and unrecognisable, the beef was tough, and there were hardly any vegetables. They all took jars of their favourite kuchela, hot pepper sauces, and any pickles they could to the canteen to make the food more palatable. It was hard to survive on custard alone.

The people of St. Vincent, like many of their Caribbean neighbours, call their staple vegetables 'ground provisions'; these include tuberous vegetables like cassava, yams, sweet potatoes and *yuka*. *Yuka* is to Caribbean cooks what the potato is to the Irish. They make flour from the root, known commonly as tapioca, which is used as a thickening agent in soups and stews, added to fruit puddings or mixed with coconut milk as a dessert. Unripe plantains and breadfruit are used as a vegetable, and when ripe as a fruit in a plethora of dishes. Now that Caribbean cooking is popular these ingredients can be found in ethnic stores and supermarkets:

Mum used to travel to Southall to get rice or Shepherds Bush to get plantain and coconut but now our corner stores have them. The Afro-Caribbean markets were great because rather than make do mum could cook what she knew best with ingredients she had when she was a kid. It made it easier for her to teach me along the way. I was definitely brought up on foods with a Caribbean flavour and wouldn't swap them for anything else. Salt fish cakes, macaroni pie with egg and loads of cheese, mango kuchela, fried plantain, and ginger beer that is so fiery it takes the roof off your mouth but still leaves you wanting more. These are the flavours of the Caribbean.

Contents of a Caribbean Store Cupboard

Curry Powder
Jerk Seasoning
Hot Pepper Sauces
Ginger
Star Anise
Chilli Powder
Scotch Bonnet Chilli
Jamaican Hot Chilli
Paprika
Pimento or Allspice
Nutmeg
Cloves
Cinnamon

Plantain
Yam
Potatoes
Cassava
Dasheen Leaves
Bay Leaves
Mint
Coriander
Garlic
Tomatoes, tinned & fresh
Onions
Black-eyed Peas
Gungo Peas or Pigeon Peas
Okra
Plantain

Canned Palm Hearts
Salt Cod
Vegetable Oil
Coconut Milk
Sugar Cane Syrup
Evaporated Milk
Potato Flour
Cornmeal Flour
Cassava Flour
Bananas
Papayas
Mangos
Passionfruit
Limes
Lemons
Angostura Bitters
Ginger Beer
Rum

Lessons learnt along the way...

People from the Caribbean have a relaxed attitude to food. They eat at all hours of the day and night, snacks frequently turning into meals. There may be the usual 'elbows off the table' rule but eating with your fingers is fine, gnawing bones until they crunch is perfectly acceptable, and dousing your food with pepper sauce and chilli before tasting it rarely offends the chef.

Caribbean dining conventions stem from the daily routine in the native countries of the inhabitants – often dictated by the heat. People get up very early in the morning and stoke up for the day on fried fish, perhaps with some rice. They may grab some fruit during the morning for a small sugar boost and to freshen the palate. The ideal is to have a larger lunch that is burnt off throughout the day but the reality is that most eat a small lunch because of the heat. It is when the sun goes down at about 5pm and the temperature drops that people start to eat. Whether it is sunny or not the aim is to have both main meals by 6pm giving the body time to digest them and relax before crashing out for the night. Later snacks might include a fried bake or a chicken wing, something tasty and usually savoury to fill up on, rather than a sweet treat.

Traditional families try to eat together, at least on Sundays, still the sacred day of rest for the more religious. The structure of a Caribbean family meal begins with soup, though only in winter. The cook plates each meal from all the pans on the stove and brings it to the table. This works particularly well with a large family because everyone gets some-thing of everything and the cook needn't worry about running out of food. Everyone is, of course free to help themselves to what remains in the pans.

Desserts are usually based on fresh fruit or coconut, often laced with Sunset rum. Coconut tarts, sweet potato pie, *docuhna* (a sweet potato fudge wrapped in banana leaf), fudge and peanut cakes are favourites. Then there are fruit and vegetable fritters accompanied by drinks like homemade chocolate, sorrell, peanut punch, black fruit wine, golden apple juice (made from a fruit that is more like a large plum with spiky seeds inside), or lime juice.

If there is cause for celebration more food is cooked than it is possible to imagine eating.

You'll have 'pick up chicken' and saltfish cakes and salce. You might even have a whole pig depending on how big the celebration is. At home they still say they will 'kill a pig for the party', which means that they will come loaded with gifts that they bring along. You'll have what we call provisions: soft yam and hard yam, tamya, plantain, sweet potatoes, cassava, then greens like Callaloo.

Large trestle tables are put out and a massive spread is laid out for everyone to help themselves:

There are always those who stick by the buffet all party long! I know I am going to eat the good stuff, all the foods that I love, when I get invited to a wedding or Christening. It's a great incentive to attend all those family occasions I might otherwise think dull. The onus for cooking never lies solely with the hostess. People bring the dishes they cook best. Some take black cake, others who are expert at rotis take massive piles of them wrapped in foil. As a kid the important part of the celebration was the food as I couldn't drink yet and I had a thing about dancing in front of people. It changes as you get older, parties become more about drink, dancing and making friends, although I have to say for me it is still all about the food!

Although notoriously generous with portions Caribbean cuisine can be simple and nutritious. It is mostly cooked on top of the stove and certain equipment is used to achieve the best results:

Apart from the roti platter, known as a 'tava', you've got to have a special pan, a 'brown down' pot, basically a special stewing pot made of iron. You put oil and sugar in it, then put it over the flame; you get it to the right temperature and consistency, then you get your meat in and 'brown it down'.

The Caribbean relies heavily on fish and seafood as staples but in western countries meats and poultry are preferred. Many favourite Caribbean foods are fried and unfortunately Type 2 diabetes is fast becoming a major killer of Caribbean people at home and abroad. A balanced Caribbean diet could be achieved if people went back to the more authentic style of eating, relying on ground provisions for bulk, legumes for protein, fruit and vegetables to add diversity and flavour, lots of fish, and red meat or poultry on the odd occasion. The best cooks in the Caribbean community are said to be the older women.

"Mum improvises, a bit of this and a bit of that but she always knows what will make something taste good but still keep it healthy. It's all in here (points to her head), instinctive. When she cooks, she feels it."

Perhaps it is they who really do know better than any finger licking fried chicken boss ever could.

In this chapter I have recreated recipes with memories and taste so that you can transport yourself to sunny climes. Improvise with them, add a little bit of this and a little bit of that until you have it right in your own head and your palate. Until you feel it!

Calalloo Soup

Mango Kuchela

Salt Fish Cakes

Rice an' Peas

Curry Goat

Fried Bake or Jo'nny Cakes

Recipes

Plantation Cinnamon Beef

Roti Skins

Pan Fried Red Snapper with Mango
Avocado Salsa

Cook Up, Boileen or Pepper Pot Stew
with Herb Dumplings

Coconut Curried Prawns

Black Cake

Calalloo Soup

The tender leaves of the dasheen plant, known as *calalloo*, make the base for this delicious and filling soup.

Pig's tail, salt meat and whole crabs are put in the meateater's version. Using salt meat rather than fresh meat adds a depth to the dish, but if you can't find salt meat on sale then you can prepare it yourself in advance: simply coat a piece of well marbled beef or pork with coarse sea salt, put in a wooden, ceramic or plastic bowl (never metal), cover and leave in the fridge overnight. Soak for at least 15 minutes before using to release some of the salt but not all. Use well-marbled meat because there is no point in salting the best lean cuts as they will dry out too quickly. A hunk of shin of beef or some rich pork belly would be perfect. If you leave the meat for up to a week you will also have home cured beef and ham – yes it really is that easy.

Serves 6

1 tin of calalloo	1.8 litres of water
8 okra	250g salt beef or pork belly (optional)
1 large onion	
1 tbsp butter	2 crabs or a medium tin of crab meat (optional)
1 hot green chilli	
1/2 tsp angostura bitters	Hot pepper sauce or chilli oil for garnish

PREP:

1 Finely chop the okra and onion

2 In a separate large pot, boil the salt meat for 15 minutes to remove excess salt

3 Clean the crabs or prepare the crab meat by chopping it into chunks

COOK:

1. In a large saucepan melt the butter and fry the chopped okra, calalloo and onion. Add 1 cup of water and simmer for 20 minutes

2. Add the salt meat, crabs or crab meat, chilli, angostura bitters, and the rest of the water

3. Simmer on a low heat for 1 hour and 20 minutes

4. Remove whole crabs and blend the soup in a blender

5. Break up the crabs into smaller pieces and put the meat back into the soup

6. Serve piping hot with a dash of hot pepper sauce or a whirl of chilli oil on top

I just love its bright green colour; it tastes and feels so healthy.

Mango Kuchela

This is the Caribbean version of the well-known Indian mango chutney introduced to the Caribbean by indentured workers. The addition of strong chilli peppers and garlic gives the sauce more heat and body than the original version. It is exceptional when served with cold meats. A spoonful also adds spice and oomph to patties or fried bakes.

4 mangoes (or one large tin, drained)	1 tsp *anchar massala* or curry powder
1 clove of garlic	2 tsp salt
2 small hot red chillies	

PREP:

1 Peel and grate the mangoes, squeezing out most of the juices

2 Spread out the paste on a rimmed baking tray

3 Mince garlic and chillies together

COOK:

1. Bake the mango paste in an oven on the lowest heat for 3 hours, stirring occasionally to mix the more caramelised parts with the rest to ensure even sweetness and colour

2. Combine the cooked mango with garlic, chilli, *anchar massala* (or curry powder) and salt to taste. Cook for 1 hour more

3. Allow to cool and serve or keep in a sterilized jar or bottle until needed.

This is a condiment made from mangos and peppers that makes it possible to eat anything... it was a sad day when I opened my luggage to find the bottle of kuchela my uncle made for me in St.Vincent had broken - a very sad day indeed!

Salt Fish Cakes

Salt Fish Cakes

These are extremely moreish. They are not fragrant like Thai fishcakes, but pack a heady chilli punch. I have tasted some with so much chilli that my eyes watered and others where it serves as a delicate backdrop. You can experiment with batches to see how strong you like yours. You can now buy salt cod from the Caribbean sections of major supermarkets and in Caribbean stores, but if you can't find it and want to get a similar effect on your own it is quite simple: pack whatever white fish you prefer, a fleshier heavy fish is best, in a few handfuls of coarse sea salt making sure all the flesh is covered and place in a plastic container. Leave in a cool place for 24-48 hours, then refresh the fish by rinsing off the salt and soaking it for 30 minutes. Serve with mango *kuchela* as a starter, snack, or light lunch with a salad, or in a Jo'nny cake on the run!

Makes 20 approx

150g salted codfish (or other white fish)	2 tomatoes
100g flour	1 clove of garlic
200ml water	2 spring onions
½ tsp paprika	1 scotch bonnet chilli
½ medium onion	

PREP:

1 Soak the salt fish in water overnight (or for at least 3 hours) to remove excess salt

2 Use a sharp knife to shred finely, making sure there are no remaining bones

3 Finely chop onions, garlic, chilli, and tomatoes

COOK:

1. In a frying pan use a small amount of oil to fry the chopped seasoning. Allow to cool

2. In a large bowl blend flour and cold water until you have a thin batter. Add paprika, the flaked fish and the cooled, fried seasoning. Mix well

3. Heat the remaining oil ready for deep frying

4. Use a wet tablespoon to pick up patties of the batter. With damp fingers flatten them a little so they will cook through and gently slide them off the spoon into the oil

5. Fry in batches so that the temperature of the oil stays constant, until they are golden brown, flipping them over half way so they are crisp on both sides

6. Drain on paper towels and serve warm

This was my grandmother's business: muffins and salt fish cakes. On Tuesdays and Wednesdays - banana days, when everyone was really busy getting the bananas cut and wrapped and prepared and ready to be shipped off, people did not have time to stop for long to cook so my granny used to go down to the port and sell her famous muffins and salt fish cakes. There were always lots of visitors at the port: seamen, traders as well as the locals, so she did really good business. I'm glad about that because it meant mum made them for us when we were growing up

Rice an' Peas

Rice an' peas is a great staple intrinsically linked with Caribbean food. Even the way it is pronounced helps us classify it as such. You will have gathered by now that most Caribbean food is actually pretty rich as well as fresh and tasty and the accompaniments are no exception. This combination of carbohydrate and protein is so filling it puts meat on bones, as our lovely grandmothers might say. Many people in the Caribbean would have at least one serving of this a day, if not more. Despite being rice and beans it is not what you might call 'healthy and light' in the calorie conscious minds of many cooks today. But the flavours of the coconut milk, herbs and spices are sublime and well worth it.

250g long-grain white rice	2 sprigs thyme
250g black eyed peas (or gunga beans or red kidney beans)	1 stick cinnamon
	1/2 tsp nutmeg
400ml chicken stock	Salt and pepper
1 can coconut milk	

PREP:

1 Wash rice well under cold running water

2 Make up 400ml chicken stock from cubes, if not using fresh stock

COOK:

1. Place the rice in a pan and cover with double the volume of chicken stock and half the can of coconut milk

2. Bring to the boil and add thyme, cinnamon, nutmeg, salt and pepper

3. Reduce the heat, cover and simmer for 15 minutes

4. Add the beans and cook for a further 5 minutes then turn off the heat

5. Stir in the rest of the coconut milk and let it sit, covered, for 15 minutes

6. Stir it with a fork to fluff the grains, pull out the cinnamon stick and thyme stalks and serve

Curry Goat

This is a popular dish at the Notting Hill Carnival in London: lots of the stalls sell it as 'authentic' goat, but they usually use autumn lamb or mutton. All are good. Just remember to buy a cut of meat that is well marbled rather than a lean fillet and don't trim it too much as the slow cooking melts all the fats, adding flavour and depth to the curry. The meat will fall apart in your mouth at the end of the long slow cooking. Caribbean timing is needed for this recipe so sit back, relax, and have a rum punch while it cooks.

I find that one of the best ways to marinate meat is in a plastic bag as you can massage it from the outside of the bag and not lose any marinade on your hands or spoons. You can do it each time you open the fridge. Really working in the flavours makes all the difference to a dish like this. Perfect with rice an' peas or scooped up with *roti* skins.

1kg goat, mutton or lamb	A small bunch of coriander roots or stems
4 tsp curry powder	3 bay leaves
2 tbsp freshly crushed pimento or allspice	3 tomatoes
Generous grating of nutmeg	Black pepper
3 cloves of garlic	3 tbsp oil
1/2 cinnamon stick, roughly broken	1 scotch bonnet chilli
2 tbsp grated ginger	50g butter or margarine
1/2 onion	700ml lamb or chicken stock

PREP:

1 Cut the meat into large cubes, place in a bowl or plastic food bag with all the dry spices; add the crushed garlic, ginger and finely chopped onion, chilli, coriander root, and chopped tomato

2 Massage the flavours into the meat and leave in the fridge to marinate for at least 2 hours, overnight if possible

COOK:

1. Melt the butter in a large pan and add the meat, browning it in batches if necessary

2. Once all the meat has been browned spoon out onto a plate

3. Add any remaining marinade to the pan and cook until the onions soften

4. Put back the meat, stir, and add the stock

5. Bring to the boil then cover and reduce the heat to a delicate simmer for 2 1/2 to 3 hours, or until the meat is tender and falls apart easily

6. Check it every 30 minutes, season to taste, and add more stock if it is drying out

7. The curry should be thick and dark when ready to serve

Fried Bake or Jo'nny Cakes

The lack of ovens in Caribbean kitchens has led to the adaptation of many traditionally baked dishes to the stovetop. Fried bakes, or *Jo'nny cakes* as they are also known, are those tasty comfort foods made by mothers and grandmothers to put flesh on bones and keep you going, hence the name. Jo'nny is not the name of the chef who created them but is derived from 'journey' – if you say 'journey' in a Caribbean accent you can see how. So these 'journey cakes' were made to fuel you on your travels.

They are good as simple snacks to take on the road, or as part of a packed lunch, or eaten with curry or soup.

450g flour	2 tsp sugar
2 tsp baking powder	300ml milk
1 tsp salt	Seed oil for frying
8 tbsp butter	

PREP:

1 In a large bowl sift the flour, baking powder, and salt

2 Cut in the butter and add the sugar

3 Mix with a fork until well combined

4 Add the milk gradually, to make a smooth dough; then knead gently

5 Cut the dough into 4-6 pieces and roll each piece into a ball

6 Let the dough rest for about 30 minutes

COOK:

1. Flatten the balls of dough in the palms of your hands to about 2cm thick

2. Coat a large pan with oil and heat over a medium flame

3. Place the *Jo'nny cakes* in the pan and fry gently for 15 minutes, turning half way through, so that the dough cooks through but remains light and fluffy inside but brown on the outside

4. Serve while still warm

Some people make a really heavy dough and some make a light one. Like my grandmother I prefer the lighter ones. That way I feel better when I stuff them with fish or cheese.

Plantation Cinnamon Beef

Plantation beef is a special Sunday meal for the family after church. Dark, heavy and wonderfully fragrant the cinnamon and nutmeg smells fill the air, whetting the appetite while the stew gently bubbles.

It is important to choose the best possible beef for the best results but this does not mean buying the most expensive cuts. Shin, top rump, chuck steaks or leg are the best cuts for slow cooking. Spices work to tenderise the meat and well marbled, slightly fatty meat will give you a thick, rich *jus*, something to remember before you pick up the neatest, cleanest pre-packaged cut in the supermarket. The finished dish will be enriched by the gelatine and melted sinew in the meat, so stir regularly to make sure this is really well distributed. It is also important to brown the meat so that the natural sugars caramelise, adding colour and flavour to the stew.

Serves 4

3 cloves of garlic	1 tbsp black peppercorns
1 onion	8 cloves
2 chillies	4 bay leaves
½ nutmeg	500g beef
5 cinnamon sticks	100ml oil for browning
2 tbsp allspice	1 litre beef or chicken stock

PREP:

1 Create a marinade by finely chopping the garlic, onion and chillies

2 Grate the nutmeg and pound it in a pestle and mortar with 3 of the cinnamon sticks, half the peppercorns and the allspice

3 In a bowl, mix the beef with the finely chopped garlic, onion and chillies, bay leaves, cloves, and the rest of the cinnamon sticks whole

4 Allow to marinate for between 2 and 24 hours

COOK:

1. Heat the oil in a pan, add the meat with the rest of the spice marinade, and brown well coating the meat in the spices and sealing in the flavours

2. Add the beef stock, bring to the boil, then cover

3. Either transfer the pan to the oven or pour the contents into a casserole dish, cover and slow cook in the oven on a low heat for 2½ hours or until the beef falls apart between your fingers. You can also do this on the hob: simply reduce the heat, using a diffuser if you have one, to a very gentle simmer for 2½ hours

4. Serve with *roti* skins or rice

Roti Skins

Roti skins were brought to the Caribbean by Indian indentured workers. The recipe has not changed greatly over time. Some prefer simple flour *rotis*, others split pea and flour *rotis*. They are not difficult to make but in the Caribbean, and now elsewhere in the world, they are also readily available from bakeries and stores. The skins are cooked on what is known as a *tawah*, which is a completely flat heavy based round pan that was created to put on a fire, but it is just as easy to use a frying pan.

170g flour	60g split peas
1 tsp baking powder	1 tsp cumin seeds
450g margarine	1 tsp salt
200ml cold water	Vegetable oil

PREP:

1 Sift the flour and baking powder into a bowl

2 Rub in the margarine

3 Add the cold water, a tablespoon at a time to bind the dough

4 Knead until smooth, not sticky

5 Cover the dough and leave in a warm place for 30 minutes

6 Prepare the split peas by cooking until tender on the outside but firm in the middle (about 25 minutes). Let the water boil away so they do not absorb too much of it. When they are cooked, spread them out on a plate or clean surface to cool

COOK:

1. Heat a clean, dry frying pan and throw in the cumin seeds; shake the pan so the seeds burst. They are ready once the aroma is released

2. Once the peas have cooled, mash them with the toasted cumin seeds

3. Knead the dough again for 3-4 minutes and divide it into four equal portions

4. On a floured surface roll out the portions into rounds, spread a tablespoon of the split peas over each round, and fold in the edges

5. Lightly brush each one with a little vegetable oil, form into balls again and leave to rest, covered, for 15 minutes

6. Roll out into thin 20cm rounds

7. Bake on a moderately hot *tawah* or a large flat frying pan. Brush one side of the *roti* with oil and cook for about one minute. Coat the other side with oil, turn it over, and cook for another minute. Keep flipping them until they are brown all over

8. Remove from the *tawah* and serve immediately or wrap in foil ready to be used when needed

Pan Fried Red Snapper with Mango Avocado Salsa

This is a really fast, fresh way to serve red snapper adding a little spice to lift the flavours but not over-powering the taste of the sweet, delicate flesh of the fish, which is perfectly complemented by the fruit.

The Caribbean pimento snapper is distinguished by smaller yellow eyes and a paler belly than the red snapper most commonly found but they taste very similar. It can also be prepared as a barbecue dish as the salsa is made in advance and will continue to marinate and macerate, the sweet juices combining with the sour lime, cutting the heat of the chilli. The fish holds together well so can be barbecued over an open grill or wrapped in foil and placed on the fire.

1 large red snapper	2 avocados
50g flour	1 chilli or 1 tsp Tabasco
1 tsp allspice or pimento	1 lime
Salt and pepper	50g butter
1 clove of garlic	Chilli sauce
1 mango	

PREP:

1 Wash and clean the fish

2 On a plate mix the flour with the freshly ground allspice, salt and pepper

3 Coat the fish in the seasoned flour

4 Crush the garlic

5 Prepare the salsa by finely chopping the chilli and combining it with the cubed mango and avocado, draining off any excess juice. Squeeze in the juice of half a lime and stir

COOK:

1. Melt the butter in a pan

2. Fry the garlic, then lay the fish in the butter, gently frying it on both sides spooning the butter over it so the skin is crisp and the flesh inside succulent.

3. Squeeze over the rest of the lime juice and a dash of chilli sauce to taste. Serve with fresh mango and avocado salsa

TIP:
Red snapper must be descaled before it is cooked. If you have to do this at home, place the fish in a plastic bag and use the back of a knife against the grain to scrape it. It is still a messy job but the bag will stop most of the scales from flying too far.

Cook Up, Boileen or Pepper Pot Stew with Herb Dumplings

Cook Up, Boileen or Pepper Pot Stew with Herb Dumplings

This dish has its origins in the ancient hunting days of the Arawak Indians, the first Caribbean peoples. The men were hunters and the women gatherers. They would keep a great pot simmering over a low fire all the times, adding the meat they caught and vegetables that became available. The stock would become more and more intensely flavoured as the pot was replenished with ingredients as and when they were caught or dug up. Nowadays, it is made using a wide range of fresh vegetables: carrots, cauliflower, peas, yam, plantain, potato, sweet potato and pumpkin, along with dumplings, stock and seasoning, and any left over meat.

Serves 6

1 onion	Water
2 cloves of garlic	Any combination or all of the following:
1 tin coconut milk	
3 large tomatoes	1 carrot, ½ cauliflower, 1 yam, 1 plantain, 1 potato, 2 sweet potatoes, ½ pumpkin
1 stem thyme	
1 scotch bonnet pepper	
200g gungo or black-eye peas	

PREP:

1 Chop the onion, crush the garlic with a little coarse sea salt, and take the thyme leaves off the stalk

2 Peel your chosen vegetables and chop them into large pieces

COOK:

1. Bring the water to the boil then add the gungo or black-eye peas. Cook until soft, drain, and set aside

2. In another pot, fry the onion, garlic, thyme, and any meat you are using

3. Add the vegetables, tomatoes, coconut milk or cream, and pepper, with enough water to ensure the liquid completely covers the vegetables

4 Bring the cook-up to a rolling boil, then lower the heat, cover and simmer for 25 minutes

5. Add the peas to the pot along with the dumplings (see left) and simmer for a further 10 minutes

Herb Dumplings

110g wholemeal flour	1 tsp fresh chives	Cold water
1 tsp baking powder	1 tsp fresh thyme	
20g margarine	1 tsp fresh coriander	

PREP:

1 Sift the flour and baking powder into a bowl

2 Rub in the margarine until well blended

3 Finely chop the fresh herbs and add to the mixture

4 Blend with sufficient cold water to bind the ingredients and produce a soft dough

5 Allow the dough to rest for about 30 minutes

6 Lightly knead the dough on a floured surface until smooth

7 Divide the mixture into 6, and shape into dumplings

COOK:

1. Drop the dumplings into the soup or boiling water for about 10 minutes

Because it has so much in it, 'cook up' is really a whole meal rather than a starter soup. My mum knew it was good for us and we knew it was good for us but because it was so tasty it didn't seem like health food. This was one of the few dishes in which I would really enjoy vegetables, although most of my time was spent playing hunt the dumpling.

Coconut Curried Prawns

Fresh fat prawns and coconut milk create a curry made in Caribbean heaven. The trick is to use the thicker coconut cream that rises to the top of the can. Make sure you don't shake the can or it will be lost. I have suggested a can of coconut milk rather than just coconut cream as the lighter coconut milk is better than stock or water to 'lengthen' the curry to a more liquid consistency. I find one can serves both purposes perfectly.

200g prawns	1 scotch bonnet chilli
1 small red bell pepper	1 tsp curry powder
2 cloves of garlic	1 can coconut milk
A small bunch of spring onions	A small bunch of coriander
5cm of ginger	Salt and pepper

PREP:

1 Clean, peel and de-vein the prawns

2 Finely chop red pepper, garlic, spring onion, ginger and chilli

3 Do not shake the can of coconut milk, open and spoon off the heavier coconut cream from the top of the can and set aside the rest of the coconut milk

4 Roughly chop the coriander

COOK:

1. Heat a little oil and fry the red pepper, garlic, spring onion, ginger and chilli with the curry powder and a pinch of salt and pepper until soft and glossy

2. Toss in the prawns and cook for one minute

3. Add the coconut cream and half the milk. Turn up the heat to cook the prawns and reduce the sauce. Add milk until you get the consistency you want

4. Cook for 10 minutes and serve with freshly chopped coriander

Black Cake

Black cake is something that all West Indians love. Usually it is made in the Christmas season and given as a present to relatives and friends but it is equally popular as a wedding or christening cake. As with English fruit cake, it takes time to make: a week is the minimum, a couple of months the norm. The better the quality of the rum used to soak the fruit and the darker the sugar, the blacker and richer the cake will be. I enjoy a really spicy cake so am generous with the cinnamon and nutmeg; add some ground ginger for even more punch. If you can't find liquid molasses, treacle can be used. The smell that emanates from the oven while it is cooking is wonderfully intoxicating!

100g exotic dried fruit (mango, papaya, pineapple, red cherries)	2 tsp vanilla essence
	2 tsp almond essence
50g raisins or currants	175g flour
20g chopped dates	1 tsp baking powder
500ml dark rum	2 tbsp ground cinnamon
110g softened butter	40g chopped pecan nuts or walnuts
30g liquid molasses or black treacle	1 heaped tsp ground nutmeg
120g firmly packed dark brown sugar	1 tsp ground cloves
	½ tsp salt
3 eggs	Icing sugar

PREP:

1. Finely chop the dried fruit and place in a large bowl
2. Pour over enough rum to cover the mix, cover and allow to stand overnight, or in a refrigerator for at least 1 week, stirring daily
3. Butter and flour the sides of a cake or square loaf tin, or line it with greaseproof paper
4. Preheat the oven to 180°C
5. In a bowl, beat the butter, molasses and brown sugar until soft and fluffy
6. Beating all the time add the eggs, one by one, then the vanilla and almond extract
7. Drain the fruit, reserving any leftover rum for adding later
8. Sift together the dry ingredients, then add to the sugar/butter mix with the leftover fruit rum (about 5 tbsp)
9. Beat the mixture until all the ingredients are combined
10. Fold in the soaked fruit and chopped nuts

COOK:

1. Put the mix into the prepared cake tin and bake for 55 minutes or until a toothpick or skewer inserted into the middle comes out clean

2. Let the cake cool in the tin for 10 minutes, then turn it out and let it cool on a wire rack until ready to serve. Dust with icing sugar and slice

Country Levain
&
Wheatgerm Levain
£2.50

A French Kitchen

Introduction to French Cuisine

French cuisine has a long, well-documented and celebrated history. The fact that we borrow their word for 'kitchen' to describe all our food and cooking demonstrates how important France has been in setting the standards for preparation and cooking ingredients, especially in Britain.

I could take you on a culinary tour of this diverse country and its *terroirs*. I could highlight the great differences in climate, produce and cuisine from the Pyrenees to the Alps, and between the Channel, the Mediterranean and the Atlantic; and the many different influences from neighbouring Latin and Saxon countries. But this is familiar ground and so what follows is an explanation of why we are so familiar with our national neighbour's eating habits and why they deserve their elevated place in the grand scheme of cuisine.

The story of French cuisine, as we know it, has its roots in Italy. In the fifteenth century the prosperity of Renaissance Florence had once again led to dining as entertainment. When Italian Catherine de Medici married the French King Henri II she brought with her a passion for life that was to inspire a new era of extravagance. Amongst her staff Catherine brought cooks who were highly skilled in bringing out the flavour of food, in its exquisite presentation, and in the use of the exceptional produce that only royalty was privy to. This was untypical at a time when cooks had to work hard to disguise poor quality foods. Dining became theatre: a spectacle for the eyes as well as a feast for the tastebuds. Henri II, keen to show his affection for his new wife acceded to her request that women would be in regular attendance at these sumptuous feasts. And they in turn indulged the appetites of the male guests by dressing in fashionable, revealing clothes. The competition to put on the greatest show on earth had begun.

Seventeenth-century French kings continued to promote their nation's excellent cuisine, demonstrating the fertility of their lands and the talent of their chefs by laying out extravagantly designed feasts of soups, game birds, vegetables, cured meats and fish, fruits and preserves. The high status of the diners and the quality and abundance of food created a new era of 'haute cuisine'. Foreign dignitaries and those aspiring to join the nobility coveted the grandeur and extravagance. They copied what they could, so much so that everyone who was anyone, across Europe at least, employed a French chef to run their kitchen. To a lesser extent this is still the case today.

The status of these grand 'home' chefs throughout the eighteenth and nineteenth centuries was akin to the popularity of today's restaurateurs/television chefs. Auguste Escoffier was yesterday's Gordon Ramsay, known in his time as 'the chef of emperors and the emperor of chefs'. Later Antonin Carême became a pioneer of design and architecture in food and enhanced the natural aesthetic by creating visual extravaganzas. Fabulous though they looked, what was displayed would most probably be cold by the time it was consumed. Guests would be invited to enter the dining room when everything was laid out; they would then sit down and serve themselves. The dishes were too elaborate to be passed round and guests could not leave their seats with the result that they could only sample those that were within reach. This continued until visiting Czars explained the Russian style of dining where separate courses were served. This was swiftly adopted in aristocratic homes across the nation where guests could look forward to twelve-course dinners. Like today's Heston Blumenthal, Anthelme Brillat-Savarin, in his book *La Physiologie du Goût* ('The Physiology of Taste'), looked at food and cuisine with a more scientific eye experimenting with taste sensations, textures and cooking methods. Brillat-Savarin, who was also a philosopher and politician, boldly stated that the destiny of a nation depended on the manner in which it fed itself. France was, therefore, by his definition destined to be the greatest nation on earth.

The extravagance of the nobility led to massive national debt and the ensuing high bread prices and high unemployment caused social unrest that ultimately led to the French Revolution. The aristocracy had their estates confiscated and across the nation hundreds of skilled chefs were suddenly out of a job. Rather than change profession – and in keeping with the tenets of the Revolution – they opened their own restaurants and offered the fruits of their labour to the masses. The high quality of the food and the equally high standards of the chefs changed the expectations of French diners and even today, most French people aspire to eat very well on a daily basis. The regions continue to develop and show off their produce and cuisine just as the aristocrats did in the past.

In the twentieth century, world travel became more common and changes in fashion led to the desire for a lighter, more delicate cuisine. The presentation and flavours of 'nouvelle cuisine', gleaned skills from the Japanese kitchen and emphasised clean lines, colour and design rather than the traditional rich sauces, intense smells and heady flavours. It was an exciting departure for French cuisine and one that again changed people's expectations, not only in France but everywhere that French cuisine was known and loved. As Paul Bocuse once said, 'Gastronomy, like any other art cannot stand still, it must renew itself'.

Throughout time, chefs like Brillat-Savarin, Escoffier, Carême and Bocuse have played an indispensable role in taking cuisine out of the kitchen and putting it on the political, scientific and artistic table for discussion.

These chefs have played their part in convincing the world of the superiority of French culinary arts but they could not have done it without the support and passion of French home cooks.

French cuisine is fiercely defended by the French today in the face of mass consumerism and competition from fast food giants. But we do not need to worry. Back at the kitchen table French food is at its strongest. Home cooks keep genuine traditions alive and proudly pass them on to new generations. The average French person – and those of French descent and Francophiles, learn to cook well from an early age and will continue to share their knowledge with all who join them for a meal.

If for no other reason, France is deserving of its reputation among the world's finest.

Flavours of a French Kitchen

Many people abroad still inaccurately associate French cooking with *haute cuisine*, foie gras with truffles or very rich sauces flavoured with garlic, onions and the traditional *herbes de Provence*. They may think French food too complex to prepare at home, with its hours of preparation and the mountains of butter needed to achieve the desired richness. But this is not the case. French flavours are more than the sum of a few ingredients:

When Maman cooked everything had a French flavour. She would cook a roast dinner and it would have a French flavour. Even when she cooked Asian food, somehow it would take on this French style. Everything of course had to be fresh for immediate use: peppercorns were crushed on demand, vanilla pods deseeded to order so that the flavours burst on your palate. She could whip up something fabulous from creamy soups to sweet treats in no time at all.

French ingredients vary according to the the climate, agricultural produce, and combinations of herbs and spices used in the different terroirs (regions). For example, Normandy cuisine favours cream sauces on rich meats and seafood, cheeses such as Camembert, and apples made into cider or puddings. In the Alsace region the legacy of German rule has left a penchant for cured pork and sauerkraut. In the Bordeaux region Bacchus was kind and bestowed the gift of rich soils where the best vines flourish, so wine is used to create many of the region's most famous dishes including *coq au vin*. Burgundy, with its equally famous wine is home to the delicious *boeuf bourguignon*. In the south, classic Mediterranean ingredients such as tomatoes, aubergines, and peppers, together with abundant anchovies and other treasures of the sea are used in dishes such as *ratatouille*, *pipérade* and *bouillabaisse*.

Fresh bread is the staple of French diet, eaten at every meal. The typical loaf – the *baguette* – contains no fat and goes stale rather quickly, so to ensure that fresh bread is available for every meal *boulangeries* are found on almost every street corner. Outside France we rarely have this luxury so bakers have begun to include butter or oil in their bread making it much less good for the figure.

Bread goes beyond the *baguette* of course. Lionel Poilâne, a Parisian baker is now known worldwide for his distinctively marked sourdough, crusty loaf. *Pain de mie* has added butter and milk, is baked in a tin, sliced and used for delicious *tartines* – slices of bread and butter. The *ficelle* is a delicate, thin baguette, the *bâtard* an oversized one. Then there is *pain de campagne* and *pain complet* flavourful rustic loaves that use rye flour and sourdough as well as wholegrain wheat. Sweet brioche baked with lots of eggs and sugar is served for breakfast, as is *pain d'épices* – lightly flavoured yeast-risen bread with warming spices such as cinnamon and nutmeg, the sweet, butter-rich *pain au chocolat*, and the ubiquitous croissant.

The flours used for baking vary across the country. The famous black *farine de blé* from Normandy makes delicious savoury *galettes*, while the strong white flours grown further south are used for the traditional *baguette*.

The renowned grey sea salt also known as Celtic Salt comes from Brittany and 'flaky sea salt' known as 'finishing salt', especially useful in cooking because it dissolves and disperses quickly, comes mainly from the southern Camargue. Apparently French sea salt contains less sodium chloride than other European salts so it is actually better for you, another factor in the 'French paradox' to be explained later.

What better to accompany fresh bread than cheese and wine – two of France's proudest achievements. Unfortunately, it is not possible to do them justice here. Suffice it to say that both are consumed daily by most French people, at home and abroad.

Perhaps it is simply because it has a French name that a *croque monsieur* commands more respect than a ham and cheese toastie; and that when a fried egg is added on top to make it a *croque madame*, it can be found on the menu of some of the most exclusive bistros.

The third on the list of the most consumed French products must be *pâté*, which was traditionally made in French country households by farmers' wives who had to make quick use of the abundant meat after the annual winter slaughter or during the shooting season to tide them over in more frugal times. After the hams and sausages, *pâtés*, *parfaits* and *terrines* were crafted from the off-cuts and often blended with vegetables, herbs and spices.

Piquancy is important to the French palate and is reflected in the condiments used: an abundance of shallots, wine and cider vinegar, as well as mustard and tarragon sauces are the most popular dressings for meat and salads. Along with dressings, French cuisine is heavily concentrated on two types of sauce: *béchamel* and *velouté*. *Béchamel* is made with butter, flour and milk; *velouté* with butter, flour and stock. It is impossible to make good stock for sauces, soups or stews without the addition of a *bouquet garni* – a bundle of herbs including parsley, thyme and dried bay leaves, sometimes tied together with string between two pieces of celery.

So we have come full circle back to those basic ingredients that constitute French flavour. Whatever they are, it is the balance of the food and the combinations of ingredients and sauces that enhance, clarify and enrich the taste of classic French food at home.

Contents of a French store Cupboard

Anchovies

Garlic

Black Peppercorns

Rosemary

Thyme

Parsley

Anise

Fennel

Tarragon

Marjoram

Bay Leaves

Dried *Herbes de Provence*

Artichokes

Onions

Shallots

Tomatoes

Lemons

Prunes

Olives

Cornichons

<u>Mushrooms</u>:
Girolles, Chanterelles, Morilles

Truffles

Dijon Mustard

Red and White Wine Vinegar

Stocks

Olive Oil

Nut Oil

Butter – salted and unsalted

Goose Fat

Cheeses

Cream

Eggs

Almonds

Chocolate

Foie Gras

Confit de Canard

Pâté

Potatoes

Puy Lentils

Haricot Beans

Haricots Verts (French beans)

Fresh Bread

Brioches and Croissants

White and Red Wine

Armagnac

Lessons learnt along the way...

Despite the history of French cuisine being dominated by chefs of note and notoriety, travel anywhere around this diverse country and you will find hearty home cooking that rivals restaurant cuisine. There is a constant debate as to whether restaurant cuisine copies and refines home cooking or home cooking simplifies restaurant cuisine. Either way, the French share a seriousness about food and a sense of pride that is almost unrivalled. The average French man or woman may not indulge in the sophisticated 'saucery' of Chez Maxim but they understand it.

A fundamental knowledge of the techniques of food preparation and cooking is inherent in most French cooks. Traditional home cooks do not tolerate short-cuts; perhaps that is why fast food is so abhorrent a concept to them. It is also apparent that the French know their ingredients and search out those that are freshest and of the highest quality:

I grew up in Somerset and Maman would always try to shop at grocers and butchers. In fact when we moved in Maman had a panic attack and wanted to move out because we had to go seven miles to find a fresh cabbage. Things have changed a little but we are really lucky in Somerset because we still have good butchers and you know where your meat and vegetables have come from. That is really important to us. Even though I live in London, I have picked up her habits of using organic food whenever possible. Nothing is pre-packaged, pre-chopped, pre-washed or powdered. I even buy peppercorns rather than pepper so it is all very fresh.

Ask any French man or woman about an artichoke and nine times out of ten, not only will they tell you where and when to get them, they will tell you how to choose the best ones and probably give you a recipe or two.

Knowledge of food is not considered specialist knowledge; it is, as it should be, general knowledge.

"The thing is... Maman has a real flair for cooking and a flair for understanding food. I think I have a sense of that too and a lot of it comes from just being around her. She never really taught me how to cook and certainly never made me cook; all my knowledge comes from assimilation. I have unconsciously studied her and French food all my life.

Since French food is considered very rich, using heart-attack-inducing quantities of butter, cheese and animal fats the slender frames of most French women remain the envy and subject of scrutiny of many nations (especially the Americans who don't understand how one can eat three times and day, often with wine, and still stay slim). Several books have been written on this phenomenon, known as the *French Paradox*. The answer most French women will give you is that it is thanks to their attention to quality and pleasure, not avoidance or deprivation.

You should take delight in life and enjoy food.

Eat it in moderation paying attention to *la ligne* (the figure) and you need never ban another food. This also applies to the flavouring and construction of meals.

Breakfast is usually sweet and nourishing, a bowl of hot chocolate and some brioche.

Lunch would be meat, vegetables and salad but because of English canteen or school packed-lunch systems I usually had something lighter like salad or a sandwich. A 'petit goûter' (sweet snack) is normal at around 4pm when children get home from school. For me this was usually chopped-up fruit with sugar sprinkled on it. *Dinner would be substantial: meat and vegetables, followed by a salad and sometimes cheese and fruit.*

We never ate dinner separately. Meals together were the backbone of the family... I still hate TV dinners. It doesn't feel right being distracted from the point of dinner and there is no respect for the food... With fast food and microwave meals people have lost the sense of occasion. I was really proud of my mother's cooking and most of my friends loved coming round for dinner.

Although meals are not formal occasions some rules of etiquette still apply.

You don't eat until you have said 'bon appétit'. You eat as soon as your food is put in front of you even if Maman is serving loads of people. You don't wait because the food is at its best when first served and ultimately the food is the most important thing. Of course you would have the almost ritualistic struggle; a sort of faux battle with the hostess telling the guests to eat and the guests saying they would wait until she was seated. These unspoken rules have, I suppose, affected the way I feel about food and drink. From a very early age we had a bottle of wine on the table. We were taught to respect the alcohol as well as the food.

Respect is central. If you appreciate the food and wine you appreciate where it comes from and who has prepared it for you. The most important thing is to enjoy your food so it would be impolite to eat the whole meal without saying how delicious the food was. It shows appreciation for the chef. Maman was proud of what she cooked and thought of the meals she prepared as a gift to us.

Because food is central to French culture and society it is inextricably linked to festivities. As Catholics there were no major eating prohibitions, only fish on Fridays and Lenten variations.

Any party or name day would be celebrated with a huge buffet; vol-au-vent, pâtés, quiches and tarts; then the myriad of sweets: chocolate éclairs filled with chocolate custard, coffee religieuses, and a stunning gâteau drenched in a very alcoholic sauce.

Christmas is still the most important feast day with six courses or more. The meal lasts from one in the afternoon until six or seven in the evening:

"You begin with a seafood dish; for us this was beef tomatoes with their seeds scooped out and cut into basket shapes. Maman had crab meat sent over from France, filled the tomatoes with it and put 'crevettes' (prawns) on top. She lined them up on a big platter and decorated it with greenery and hard boiled eggs. She made her own mayonnaise and drizzled it over the whole dish. She then added chunks of cucumber with the seeds scooped out and filled with lumpfish caviar. The second course was always foie gras and fine Melba toast served with home-made jelly cut into tiny cubes. The third course was salad to prepare for the courses to come.

For the main course Maman never really went for turkey, but as she wanted to keep it a little bit English we had pheasant. When I was little, she would sit by the fire and burn the feathers off, I would only see it once its pimply skin was revealed. She roasted it with lots of garlic and rosemary from the garden. The fifth course would be cheese, always a Crottin – rich goat's cheese, some Roquefort, and a Camembert, served with French bread and biscuits. Finally there was home-made Christmas pudding, her homage to England. It was her attention to detail that I loved. She was creative and very artistic with food. Taste always came first but the food had to look beautiful too.

The French have a sweet tooth and the art of *pâtisserie* (pastry-making) is taken very seriously. Most people go to their local *pâtissier* for the famed *fraisiers*, *mille-feuilles* or *opéras* but the art is not left solely to the professionals. Cooks from all walks of life take great pride in home-made silken chocolate mousse, caramelised *tarte tatin*, tangy *tarte au citron* and much more.

I remember desserts and cakes playing a huge part in my diet growing up. I loved them. Around the festive season the kitchen was always on the go. Maman would make a fabulous Yule log: a very thin layer of sponge soaked with Grand Marnier, covered with apricot jam and a layer of vanilla cream and then rolled up. She covered the log with chocolate chestnut cream and decorated it with marzipan dyed red and green and fashioned into small toadstools and birds or made into ivy that climbed all over it.

Whether it is cakes for Epiphany, *foie gras* for Christmas or the daily *baguette*, French food is so well known and so well loved that it is available all over the world.

What you might not grasp if you don't buy from or eat with French people is their sense of passion and unnerving commitment to food. But find someone French and all you need do is ask. They will share everything with you in an instant.

Recipes

Crème de Cèpes
Cream of Cèpes

Pissaladière
French Style Anchovy and Onion Tart

Agneau en Croûte d'Herbes
Lamb with Herb Crust

Coquilles St. Jacques
Baked Scallops

Cassoulet de Canard
Duck Cassoulet

Steak au Poivre avec Pommes Frites
Steak with Pepper Sauce and French Fries

Saumon au Beurre Rouge
Pan Roasted Salmon with Red Butter

Lapin à la Moutarde
Pan Roasted Mustard Rabbit

Îles Flottantes
Floating Meringue Islands on a
Sea of Vanilla Cream with Caramel Sauce

Clafoutis de Cerises
Cherry Clafoutis

Gourmandises de Chocolat Chaudes
Warm Chocolate Gourmandises with Chocolate Sauce

Crème de Cèpes [Cream of Cèpes]

Crème de Cèpes
Cream of Cèpes

The French are famed for their magnificent soups; some are simple broths, others just blitzed up vegetables but the simplicity and elegance of the crèmes are second to none. Like the little black dress you can dress them up or down – perfect for every occasion.

The stock that goes into making the soup is as important as the quality of the ingredient itself so where possible make it yourself or buy fresh. Otherwise use a quality stock cube that is high in concentrate and low in flour and salt. The stock is infused with the dried cèpes so takes on an earthy flavour before being used as a base. If you can find fresh cèpes use them but the season only runs from July to November so at other times buy dried ones and soak them, and use other seasonal mushrooms to give the cream consistency. A fabulous way of serving this soup that takes it out of the every day is to create little 'amuse bouche' or taste ticklers. This is a pre-starter that whets the appetite and literally translated 'amuses your mouth'. Pour the soup into cups and create mini cèpe cappuccinos topped with light creamy froth and grated nutmeg.

Serves four as a starter or six as an 'amuse bouche'

250g fresh cèpes (or other seasonal mushrooms)	150ml double cream
	50g butter
2 shallots	500ml chicken stock
100g dried cèpes	Salt and pepper
1 clove garlic	
1 egg plus 1 egg yolk	

PREP:

1 Wipe the mushrooms with a damp cloth to remove all the grit, then dice

2 Peel and finely chop the shallots

3 Soak the dried cèpes in warm water for 10 minutes to remove any grit or dirt

4 In a bowl, whisk 100ml cream with one whole egg and an additional separated egg yolk

5 Whip the remaining 50ml cream until light and fluffy

COOK:

1. Bring the chicken stock to the boil in a casserole pan and add the soaked dried cèpes. Take off the heat and allow to infuse for at least 10 minutes

2. Melt the butter in a pan and sweat off the shallot, then add the diced fresh cèpes or fresh mushrooms. Toss to ensure they are all covered in butter and are cooked evenly. Using a slotted spoon drain the soaked cèpes. Keep a few for garnish and fry the rest with the fresh mushrooms in the pan

3. Put the stock back on the heat and bring to the boil; then mix in the eggy cream, whisking well

4. Add the fried mushrooms and season well to taste. Lower the heat and allow the mushroom flavour to infuse the soup. Blend to a smooth cream and warm through but do not allow the mixture to boil again

5. Taste and adjust seasoning. If it feels too thick loosen with a little stock or double cream

6. Pour the soup into four cups or small bowls, spoon over a little whipped cream and top with freshly grated nutmeg or the remaining cèpes fried

Pissaladière
French Style Anchovy and Onion Tart

Anchovies thrive in the Mediterranean sea and fishermen have been catching and preserving these delicacies for hundreds of years. When caught the fish are immediately mixed with sea salt and once ashore they are gutted, filleted and laid out, covered in more salt and allowed to mature for about three months before being packed into jars of brine. *Pissaladière* is more of a street food than home food if you live in the South of France; elsewhere it is made in batches as a great summer snack on kitchen tables. You can make one large tart or lots of small individual-sized tarts.

1 sachet dried yeast (usually 7g)	250g plain flour
	5 yellow or white onions
1 tbsp sugar	50g anchovies, salted or canned
1 tbsp milk	
1 egg	1 sprig of thyme
1 tbsp extra virgin olive oil	100g pitted black olives
1 tsp salt	4 tbsp extra virgin olive oil

PREP:

1 In a bowl mix dried yeast, sugar and milk with 125ml warm water

2 Blend in 1tablespoon flour. Leave for at least 5 minutes so it becomes frothy

3 Add the egg, oil and salt

4 Sift the flour in gradually binding the mix together, first of all with a large spoon but eventually with your hands

5 Knead the dough until it forms a firm but slightly sticky ball. Seal the top of the bowl with clingfilm and set aside for 2 hours until it has doubled in size

6 Peel and slice the onions

7 If you have salted anchovies you should rinse them before using them as a topping

COOK:

1. Heat the olive oil in a pan, add onions and thyme and sauté over a low heat until golden and soft

2. Bring out the dough and cut into four

3. On a floured surface roll or simply use your fingers to push into a roundish base, rather like a pizza

4. Preheat oven to 200°C. Grease a baking tray and bake the four bases for 6 minutes

5. Once part-cooked, top the tarts with the caramelised onions and a criss-cross pattern of anchovies dotted with black olives

6. Return to the oven and bake for 10-12 minutes

Agneau en Croûte d'Herbes
Lamb with Herb Crust

A perfectly simple Sunday lunch for the family or elegant dinner with friends on a summer evening. The olives and herbs make a deep green paste that smells and looks deliciously appetising.

Serve with peppers, courgettes and aubergines slow roasted in some good olive oil with a little garlic and thyme for a truly Mediterranean flavour.

50g pain de mie (or any crusty soda bread)	10 basil leaves
10-15 pitted black olives	1 egg
1 clove of garlic	Rack of 8 lamb cutlets
50ml olive oil	1 large knob of butter
A handful of fresh parsley	Glug of olive oil
A handful thyme sprigs	Salt and pepper

PREP:

1 Put olives, garlic, stripped thyme, basil, parsley and bread in a blender or coffee grinder, pulse until it forms breadcrumbs. If you don't have a blender, grate the breadcrumbs and garlic, finely chop herbs and olives, and mix together

2 Drizzle in a little olive oil until it becomes a firm, thick paste

3 Score the fat of the lamb in a criss-cross pattern or remove

4 Whisk the egg. Roll the lamb in it. Spread the paste over the meat with a knife or your hands. Refrigerate for 30 minutes

5 Preheat the oven to 220°C

COOK:

1. Melt the butter in a large pan and add another glug of oil to stop the butter burning

2. Fry the lamb to seal the edges and set the crust, spooning over the buttery oil to coat the meat

3. Transfer the lamb to the oven and cook for 15-25 minutes so that the centre remains a delicate pink

4. Let the meat rest for 10 minutes covered with foil. Slice into cutlets and serve with roasted vegetables

This reminds me of being at home because of the smell of herbs and garlic, quintessential French home cooking.

Coquilles St. Jacques [Baked Scallops]

Coquilles St. Jacques
Baked Scallops

From wedding celebrations to Christmas lunches Coquilles Saint Jacques are one of the most highly-rated seafoods. They are named after Saint James, whose emblem bears the scallop shell. A medieval legend claims that the brave James the Great rescued a knight who was drowning and who emerged covered in scallops; another that on a pilgrimage to Spain a horse fell into water and emerged covered in scallops. Today, as in centuries past, pilgrims on their way to the shrine of Saint James in Santiago de Compostela still wear a scallop shell around their necks.

If you can, buy hand-caught scallops, so much better for you and the environment. Unlike the mechanical trawlers that suck up everything on the ocean floor then spit out what cannot be sold, divers choose only the biggest scallops leaving the rest to grow and because they do not disturb the sea bed, less grit and impurities get into the shell ensuring a fresher, cleaner taste.

Serve simply as a starter or light lunch or combine with other seafood such as king prawns, pieces of salmon, mussels or, for a truly British twist, cockles.

1 small onion	60g butter
2 potatoes	1 tbsp plain flour
A splash of milk	Salt and pepper
A knob of butter	1 egg yolk
400ml water	65ml double cream
250ml white wine	A handful of fresh parsley
1 small bunch thyme	4 scallop shells, large
1 bay leaf	ramekins or small shallow
16 scallops	bowls that will withstand the heat of the grill

PREP:

1 Roughly chop the onion

2 Peel and boil the potatoes. Make a thick mash by adding a little milk, butter and salt to taste

COOK:

1. In a large saucepan put water, wine, thyme, onion, bay leaf, salt and pepper and bring to the boil

2. Drop in the scallops for one minute. Remove them and set aside. Boil the mixture to reduce by half, skimming off any scum

3. In another pan melt the butter and mix in the flour to make a loose 'roux'. Cook for 1 minute stirring all the time so that it doesn't burn

4. Pass the prepared wine stock through a fine sieve to remove the onion, thyme, etc. Add to the roux, stirring well so the sauce does not become lumpy

5. Once all the liquid has been stirred in, the sauce will remain very thick. Bring to the boil, then simmer for about 6 minutes to cook the flour

6. In a bowl whisk the egg yolk and cream and add to the roux gradually. Warm through

7. Evenly distribute the scallops with any other seafood in the serving dishes or shells. Spoon over the sauce, then cover with the mashed potato. Save a little mash to stick the shells to the serving dish

8. Brush melted butter over the potato. Brown under a pre-heated grill. Sprinkle with freshly chopped parsley

Cassoulet de Canard [Duck Cassoulet]

Cassoulet de Canard
Duck Cassoulet

This is a beautiful dish, a real winter warmer. It does require quite some time and preparation but they do say that the best things come to those who wait. So many ingredients can be used and it takes hours to cook in the oven but the result is sumptuous, indulgent and definitely worth all the effort.

There are several versions of cassoulet originating from south-east France. The Toulouse version, for example, uses their great sausages. Carcassone cassoulet is made with partridge but the original, said to have been created during the Hundred Years' War (14-15th century) in Castelnaudary, uses duck and sausages. Its name allegedly derived from the 'cassole' pot in which it was first made. Wherever it comes from, a good cassoulet has to include quality haricot or lingot beans, good stock and rich meats.

300g white haricot beans	300g belly pork rashers
1 large carrot	300ml dry white wine
2 celery sticks	500ml stock
4 cloves of garlic	400g (1 can) chopped tomatoes
2 large onions	1 tbsp tomato purée
8-10 cloves	Salt and pepper to taste
6 duck legs	
4 tbsp goose or duck fat (or half butter, half oil)	**For the topping:**
	1 large day-old baguette
1 bouquet garni (2 bay leaves, a few sprigs of thyme and flat leaf parsley, 1 celery stick halved, all tied together)	2 fat garlic cloves, chopped
	1 heaped tbsp fresh thyme
	A handful of flat leaf parsley
2 large sausages (beef or pork)	60g butter

PREP:

1 If the beans are dried rather than tinned soak them in water overnight then rinse

2 Peel and chop 2 garlic cloves, carrot, celery, and 1 onion

3 Stud the other onion with cloves

4 Make crumbs of the bread, parsley and thyme in a blender and fry in butter with the finely chopped garlic until they are golden brown

COOK:

1. Drain beans and place in a saucepan, cover with fresh water and add studded onion, bouquet garni and 2 garlic cloves. Simmer for 30 minutes

2. Meanwhile, pre-heat the oven to 200°C. Roast the duck legs for 30 minutes, turning occasionally

3. Fry the sausages, set aside; then fry the pork belly

4. Once the belly has browned a little, add the chopped carrot, celery and remaining garlic and continue to sauté together for about 10 minutes

5. Transfer everything except the studded onion and bouquet garni to a casserole dish, add tomato purée and chopped tomato, thyme, wine and stock

6. Bring to the boil, cover and simmer for 1½ hours

7. Remove skin from the duck, uncover and continue to simmer on a low heat or in a warm oven for 1½ hours until the sauce has thickened. Season to taste

8. Cover with golden breadcrumbs and serve

Steak au Poivre avec Pommes Frites [Steak with Pepper Sauce and French Fries]

Steak au Poivre avec Pommes Frites
Steak with Pepper Sauce and French Fries

A steak is pretty unbeatable in terms of great flavour. These days we are all health conscious so red meat is eaten in moderation but if you are going to do something then it is worth doing well. Buy the best quality steak you can afford, cook it lightly, and enjoy it with this simple sauce and a mound of salty fat chips.

In restaurants steak snobbery is not uncommon. I agree steaks are better rare and tender rather than tough and chewy but at home you do as you please and you can choose any of the following:

Bleu – Meaning 'blue'; the steak basically touches a very hot pan on both sides

Saignant – Meaning 'bloody'; 'very rare' by British standards but deliciously moist

A point – Meaning 'to a turn', or 'just done'; what the British would consider 'rare'

Bien cuit – Meaning 'well cooked'. A sacrilege for most chefs

Très bien cuit – Meaning 'very well cooked'. The usual British barbecue standard

2 large potatoes	25g butter
Oil for frying	400ml cream
Palmful of peppercorns	Generous pinch of coarse sea salt
2 sirloin or fillet steaks	

PREP:

1 Peel and chop the potatoes into fat chips

2 Crush the pepper corns roughly in a pestle and mortar or with a cup and rolling pin

3 Pre-heat the oven on low

COOK:

1. Heat a pan of oil and fry the chips until golden brown. This usually takes 20 minutes, unless you have a deep fat fryer

2. Drain the chips on kitchen paper and transfer them to a bowl. Place in the oven to keep warm, along with the serving plates

3. Melt the butter in a frying pan. When foaming add the steaks and cook to your requirements

4. Take them out of the pan and place on warmed plates to rest while you make the sauce

5. Using the same pan add the crushed peppercorns and fry until fragrant then pour in the cream and deglaze the pan picking up all the meaty juices and caramel left from the steaks. Use a spoon or spatula to make sure all the flavours are incorporated

6. Heat through for a couple of minutes, then pour over the steaks and serve with a portion of salted chips

I was always really English in the fact that I didn't like my steaks to be too rare. I wanted them well done much to my mother's chagrin. However they are cooked, with fresh pepper sauce picking up the flavours in the pan, they are delicious.

Saumon au Beurre Rouge [Pan Roasted Salmon with Red Butter]

Saumon au Beurre Rouge

Pan Roasted Salmon with Red Butter

Most people would not partner pink fish with red wine but this combination is incredible. The crisp skin of the salmon and the juicy flesh are complemented by the rich sauce rather than masked. It is important when cooking to use a good quality red wine: the better the ingredients that go into the dish the better the outcome. The only thing you have to watch with this dish is that you don't cook the butter sauce for too long as it will turn and become oily rather than silken and clean. Red butter is just as delicious with other types of heavier white fish such as hake, cod or even swordfish steak.

To balance the colour on the plate and the textures I would serve this with light, fluffy pommes mousseline (whipped mashed potato) and blanched green beans or on a bed of spinach.

4 salmon fillets	1 glass port (optional)
Sea salt and black pepper	Juice of 1/2 lemon
2 shallots	A handful of flat leaf parsley
2 large glasses dry red wine	300g butter

PREP:

1 Season the salmon fillets with sea salt and freshly crushed black pepper

2 Finely slice the shallots

COOK:

1. In a saucepan reduce the wine and port by 1/3 with the shallots

2. Add the lemon juice and chopped parsley

3. Allow to cool slightly then slowly add the butter, stirring constantly. Season to taste

4. Transfer the butter to a frying pan, heat through and place the salmon in the pan skin side down. Spoon over the red butter constantly coating the flesh and not allowing it to dry

5. Once the salmon has cooked half way up the fillet turn over carefully and continue to baste until cooked. This should take about 6 or 7 minutes in total. Be careful not to overcook the fish or let the butter turn

6. Serve immediately. The skin should be crisp and the flesh succulent

Lapin à la Moutarde
Pan Roasted Mustard Rabbit

Rabbits used to be the staple meat for farmers and rural villagers across Europe. France was no exception. The meat has for some reason fallen out of favour in the UK but is still widely enjoyed in France and other Mediterranean countries. In the same way as we usually want to know how the meat we are going to eat has been reared and whether it has had organic feed or other processed feeds it is always worth asking if the rabbit has been reared on a farm or was wild. Some rabbits will be free to roam the fields nibbling pastures and herbs but these have a wilder much strong flavour akin to hare. Farm rabbits tend to stay closer to home, are usually fed on vegetable leaves as well as nuts and seeds giving their meat a more delicate flavour.

French mustard comes in a huge variety of strengths and depths and you can try different regional varieties, wholegrain or smooth depending on your taste. I prefer a smoother texture for this dish so a classic Dijon does wonderfully. This dish is great accompanied by a creamy potato gratin.

4 cloves of garlic	Large glass of white wine
10 shallots	5 tbsp Dijon mustard
1 rabbit	500ml chicken stock
100g butter	

PREP:

1 Finely chop garlic and shallots

2 Joint the rabbit into 8 pieces

COOK:

1. Melt butter in a large casserole pan and fry the garlic and shallots

2. Brown the rabbit in stages so all the pieces are well coloured

3. Remove from the pan and deglaze it with the wine

4. Using a brush coat the rabbit in mustard and put it back in the pan

5. Add the chicken stock, bring to the boil, then cover and simmer for 40 minutes, removing any smaller pieces after 30 minutes

6. Remove the rabbit from the pan and keep warm in the oven while you reduce the remaining stock by half

7. To finish simply pour the sauce over the rabbit and serve

Îles Flottantes

Floating Meringue Islands on a Sea of Vanilla Cream with Caramel Sauce

This pudding is a home cooking classic; it flies in the face of haute cuisine as it was created to use up store cupboard ingredients. It had a burst of popularity in the 1980s and as with so many dishes from the '80s the kitsch reputation has stuck. It is usually made for children but definitely enjoyed by all. Depending on how creative you feel you can bring out your inner child by adding sugar palm trees and sea monsters.

4 large eggs	300ml milk for poaching
1 vanilla pod	Pinch of salt
25g caster sugar	
50g icing sugar	For caramel sauce:
700ml milk	25ml water to 50g sugar

PREP:

1 Separate the egg yolks from the whites

2 Split open the vanilla pod with a sharp knife and scrape out all the seeds

3 In a separate bowl whisk the egg yolks with caster sugar until a light yellow cream is formed

4 In a completely dry, clean bowl whisk the egg whites and icing sugar until they form firm peaks

COOK:

1. Pour milk into a small pan, add vanilla seeds and opened pod, warm the milk but do not let it boil

2. Take the pan off the heat and take out the pod. Pour the egg mixture gradually into the milk whisking quickly all the time so that you don't create runny scrambled eggs

3. Put the pan back on the heat and add the vanilla pod. Cook over a medium flame until the mixture is thick enough to coat the back of a spoon, whisking all the time

4. Pour into a bowl and allow to cool

5. Make the islands by scooping some meringue into a large spoon. Take another large spoon and gently transfer it from spoon to spoon to create a firmer egg shape and poach them by dropping them into 300ml of warmed milk for a couple of minutes

6. Prepare the caramel by melting the sugar and water together over a medium flame. It will burn quickly once ready so keep an eye on it

7. To serve, place the poached islands on top of the vanilla cream and pour over the caramel

Îles flottantes are heavenly. The sea is made of a vanilla cream; it is very light, less rich than proper cream but the same consistency and Maman always used real vanilla pods so it would have specs in it. She made the meringue with egg whites and lemon juice with sugar and she also made the caramel that she poured over the islands. It was She served it in glass bowls and it was absolutely spectacular.

Clafoutis de Cerises
Cherry Clafoutis

The all too brief cherry season comes after the heady spring blossoms have passed. The delicate fruit is collected from mid-May to the beginning of July. There are two main varieties: sweet and bitter. The most common of the sweet cherries is the French Bigarreau. Morello – round, deep red and sometimes black – is the best known bitter cherry. The Gean cherry is most commonly used for kirsch and liqueurs. When choosing cherries look for those that have a smooth skin and are a shiny bright colour. The stem should be bold green, supple, and firmly attached.

The unusual name *clafoutis* allegedly comes from *clafir*, a dialect word from the Limoges region meaning 'to fill'. It is rich and uses up surplus milk, eggs and fruit. It is traditionally made with black cherries, although there are other versions made according to the season: peaches, pears, prunes, apricots or grapes work well, especially when soaked in Armagnac for extra richness. The cherries are traditionally left un-pitted. The 'pits' intensify the flavour making it slightly earthier rather than overly sweet and they won't 'bleed' in the batter. Make sure your oven is really hot. This prevents the mix from separating and gives wonderful colour and crispness on the outside while ensuring a smooth filling.

400g cherries	Seeds from 1/2 vanilla pod
150ml kirsch or rum	Pinch of salt
100ml milk	3 eggs
50g flour	Icing sugar for decoration
100g caster sugar	

PREP:

1 Pre-heat the oven to 180°C

2 Butter and flour a cake tin or mould

3 In a bowl mix the cherries and the kirsch or rum and marinate for at least 20 minutes

COOK:

1. Drain the cherries – reserving any juices for later – and place them in the cake tin or serving dish. Put this in the oven until the cherries are warm

2. Meanwhile, in a bowl mix the flour, sugar and vanilla seeds with a pinch of salt

3. Whisk the eggs until smooth and add to the flour, little by little, to make a batter consistency

4. Add the milk, again little by little to make a smooth, thick batter

5. Remove the pan carefully so the cherries don't burst and 'bleed' and pour them over the batter

6. Put back in the oven for 30-35 minutes. The clafoutis should be golden on top and feel firm to the touch

7. Allow to cool a little then dust with icing sugar and serve with a small jug of any remaining cherry/kirsch juice

Gourmandises de Chocolat Chaudes
Warm Chocolate Gourmandises with Chocolate Sauce

The French passion for chocolate has never been a secret. Voltaire allegedly drank twelve cups a day while the nineteenth-century French gastronomic chronicler, Brillat-Savarin asserted, 'Chocolate is health'. He prescribed it for many ills and conditions from lethargy to hangovers. The medicinal benefits of chocolate have been confirmed by medical science but most enjoy it for the indulgent pleasure, with unfortunate ensuing guilt. Either way it has captured the taste buds of men, women and children all over the world.

Makes 8

7 eggs	20g unsweetened cocoa powder
200g caster sugar	60g butter
350g bitter chocolate (at least 70% cocoa)	150ml double cream

PREP:

1 Separate the eggs. Beat the egg whites with 120g sugar in a clean dry bowl. In another bowl beat the yolks with 80g sugar

2 Butter and flour four ramekins and leave the remaining butter so it warms to room temperature

3 Chop 100g of chocolate into small chunks

COOK:

1. Melt 250g bitter chocolate in a bain-marie then add the cocoa and gradually stir in small chunks of butter until they melt and the chocolate is shiny and silky

2. Allow the chocolate to cool a little then stir in the egg yolk mixture beating fast so the egg does not scramble. Fold in the egg white to preserve as much air as possible

3. Fill the ramekins three-quarters full with the chocolate mousse and bake in a 180°C oven for 15-20 minutes. They should be soft to the touch and a little gooey in the middle

4. While they are cooking make a simple chocolate sauce by bringing the cream to a boil then pouring it over the remaining chopped chocolate. Stir until you have a smooth consistency

5. Once the chocolate gourmandises have cooled a little turn them out, dust with icing sugar or cocoa powder and serve with the warm chocolate sauce

The first thing that came to mind when you asked about dishes from my childhood were desserts and my mother's chocolate mousse was the best of all. She was always insistent that the chocolate used was of the best quality with the highest cocoa levels.

An Indian Kitchen

Introduction to Indian Cuisine

Indian food is as rich and diverse as the country itself. From the Himalayas in the north to the desert on the Pakistani border, to the coastline of the Arabian Sea, the climate, terrain, people and their habits differ dramatically.

In the country's seven territories different religions have brought different culinary practices. The country's many cuisines do, however, share common traits: rich colours, the use of aromatic spices, interesting flavours, and a variety of ingredients.

As with most nations, history has influenced cuisine as much as geography. It is thought that the Dravidians domesticated animals and cultivated crops on a small scale as far back as 2500 BC. Sanskrit texts tell us that the *tarka* technique of throwing whole spices into hot oil or ghee was common, and apparently there is evidence of the ghee versus seed oil health debate even then. Later the Aryans ruled and grew wheat in the north and rice in the south.

As with all cuisines geography dictates ingredients and as wheat is the staple crop of the north and east of India, dishes from these regions are more likely to be accompanied by *naan*, *paratha*, *papad* or *chapatti*. Dishes from the south and east of the country are traditionally accompanied by rice, the staple in these wetter regions.

Emperor Asoka converted to Buddhism in 321 BC and the people embraced vegetarianism. Hinduism later spread and the cow headed towards semi-deification, although evidence suggests it was still widely eaten until 800 AD when the old Vedic Indian religion was challenged by the growth of Buddhism and Jainism, both of which frowned upon the killing of animals.

By 1000 AD many rulers had come and gone and left many changes to the countryside but with the invasion of the Mughals from Persia – a land famed for its diverse spices – came a huge change leading to a preference for richer, more aromatic dishes. The eating of lamb and goat grew in popularity as did the use of the spices we now think of as synonymous with Indian cuisine: saffron, cardamom, cinnamon, mace, nutmeg, and cloves. The Mughal Emperors lived in great opulence. One expression of this was the use of a multitude of dried nuts and fruit that added richness and flavour to their foods.

Perhaps one of the most recent dramatic influences on Indian cuisine was the Portuguese invasion of Goa. The Portuguese were, of course, traders as well as colonisers and when they captured the southern territory in 1510 they introduced tomatoes, peppers and, most importantly, chillis.

The British did not have the culinary clout to change the Indian diet but they did bring tea from China – it is now one of India's main export crops and most popular drinks – and popularised Indian food. The first appearance of curry on a menu was in 1773 at the Coffee House in Norris Street, Haymarket, London. The first dedicated curry house was opened in Portman Square, London in 1809 and was more conservatively known as the Hindostanee Coffee House (as recorded in *The Epicure's Almanac*).

In Britain we are so fond of Indian cuisine in all its varieties that we have taken many dishes to our hearts and consider them amongst our favourite foods.

Flavours of an Indian Kitchen

Indian cuisine is predominantly recognised by its use of spices and rich 'gravies' or sauces. The spices have three functions: to preserve food, to season it, and for their medicinal value. Seasoning is probably the most common reason for their use today. Arguments rage as to what is the most important spice in Indian cuisine so I will not try to call it. Suffice it to say that chilli, pepper, black mustard seed, cumin, coriander seed, allspice berries (also known as pimento), and turmeric are high on the list. Bay leaves as well as fresh coriander and mint are popular and in the south 'curry' leaves are commonly used, along with litres of coconut milk.

Spices are enjoyed as a snack as well as in the flavouring of foods. Different blends are served to whet the appetite, aid digestion or refresh the breath. One classic after-dinner mix called *Suwadhana* includes sunflower and sesame seeds, anise, cloves and cumin.

Two things to note about Indian flavours: when chillies are used they are always green, and turmeric is used in almost everything. Yellow fingers characterise Indian food for me because of it.

Garam masala and *anchar masala*, the basic hot and mild curry powder blends, are created from five or more dried spices and go into most dishes. Every *sabji* or *shak* begins with a basic paste, created by dry frying the spices then adding ghee or oils. Even this reflects regional roots: northern Indian cooks use mustard oil for frying while those from western India may use groundnut oil. Gujarati cooks use vegetable oil rather than ghee and Goans often use coconut oil. Once the oils have been flavoured, onions, garlic and ginger are added followed by the main bulk ingredients such as vegetables or pulses, and the sauce or 'gravy' is then made with either coconut milk, tamarind water or chopped tomatoes.

The best antidote to the hot spices of a curry is dairy products but because of the heat in India fresh milk has always been quickly turned into something else such as yogurts, cheeses and curds. *Lassi*, a runny yogurt drink flavoured with salt or fruit such as mango is consumed throughout the day and is fantastic for cutting out the 'burn' of some dishes. *Chenna*, a cottage cheese and *raita* are served fresh or with onion or mint. *Paneer*, an Indian style firm cheese can be eaten fresh or in a curry. Like chicken it provides an excellent source of protein and is a neutral-tasting base that takes on the flavours of the 'gravy'. Buttermilk is often used alongside evaporated or condensed milk in Indian sweets and desserts such as *jalebi* – syrup-filled rings made from a white flour and yogurt batter.

Indian sweets have a reputation for being just that, ultra sweet. There is a wide variety but most are made with *khova* (dried evaporated milk). *Ghee* (clarified butter), sugar and other flavours such as rose or orange oil are added, along with bright colourings. They are moulded and turned into sweets such as *barfi*, *malai*, *rasgulla*, *kheer*, and *sandesh*, decorated with ground pistachios, almonds or raisins. *Kulfi*, an Indian style ice cream is also very popular and is made with a wide variety or fruit, nuts and flowers. Puddings include *halwa* and *kheer* and – my personal favourite – sponge balls dipped in warm sugar syrup or honey called *gulab jamun*.

Contents of an Indian Store Cupboard

Allspice Berries

Aniseed

Basmati Rice

Cardamom Pods (Black and Green)

Chillies

Cinnamon

Cloves

Coconut Milk

Coconut Flesh (Dried or Fresh)

Coriander Leaves

Coriander Seeds

Cumin Seeds

Kaffir Lime Leaves

Curry Leaves

Curry Powder

Fenugreek Seeds

Garlic

Ginger

Mustard Seeds

Paprika

Tamarind

Turmeric

Limes

Tomato Purée

Fresh Tomato

Saffron Stems

Almonds

Sugar

Ghee

Vegetable Oil

Yogurt

Paneer

Onions

Mushrooms

Potato

Spinach

Chick Peas

Garam Flour

Channa Dhal (Green Lentils)

Toor Dhal (Split Red Beans)

Urid Dhal (Split Black Beans)

Lessons learnt along the way...

The Ayurvedic principles of eating are still as strong in Indian cuisine today as they were hundreds of years ago; foods are combined for health and healing properties.

The use of ingredients and spices in diet can be preventative or curative. Foods are categorised into three main groups; *satvic* (juicy, fresh and light), *rajasic* (hot, sour and salty) or *tamasic* (dry, bland, processed). Each has a certain effect upon the body and mind. The basic aim for preventative 'medicine' or to promote all-round health should be to eat more *satvic* than *tamasic* foods. In curative terms spices are prescribed for different ailments. For example, pepper is used to cure digestive ailments. A turmeric paste is applied to burns, itchy skin, etc. Ginger is a remedy for liver complaints, anaemia and rheumatism. Those suffering from nausea, fever, or headaches might be prescribed dishes or tea containing cardamom. Cinnamon mixed with honey is still one of the most potent natural cure-alls prescribed for everything from toothache to cancer.

Those who follow a strict Ayurvedic diet can eat only seasonal foods, locally grown. Eating outside these boundaries is said to 'upset the body and the Gods!' This belief is akin to the Chinese *yin* and *yang* belief that waking the spirits at the wrong time causes turbulence inside the body and in nature. With the import-export business of foods as it is today these principles are extremely hard to adhere to and, in my opinion, would make life somewhat boring. It would mean that in Britain we would never be able to eat bananas, black-eyed peas, or lentil dhal; nor could we flavour our foods with spices such as cardamom or even cinnamon.

For most Indian home cooks the foundation on which to build every meal is rice or bread, lentils, and *ghee* or oil.

These provide the three main components of a meal: carbohydrate, protein and fat. Herbs, spices, pickles and yogurts add a range of vitamins and minerals, as well as medicinal uses such as anti-inflammatory or digestive aids.

As well as health and healing, religion plays a significant part in the diet of many Indians in Britain, with fasting a common practice:

My father fasts every Thursday for spiritual reasons; he has done so for most of his adult life and other members of the family have decided to join him. Mother always prepares the same meal on a Thursday night so they can eat properly when the fast has ended.

There has been a distinct change in diet since the first generation of Indians came to Britain. For example, most Gujarati Brits today eat meat; their parents would have done so on occasion but their grandparents would never have touched it:

In most traditional Gujarati households, bearing in mind we're supposed to be strict vegetarians, and to some orthodox types this means no eggs and animal fat or produce, the main meal in the evening is the same every night; a 'shak' with different vegetables. Although it is really tasty, sometimes it just gets too repetitive and restrictive. Don't get me wrong. I wasn't an awkward child. I just prefer my meat dishes. My parents have tried so hard to get my sister and I to co-operate but when we respectively became old enough to cook for ourselves my mother gave up. To this day I still prefer a chicken tikka masala to a dhal. My mother is mortified when my sister and I are the only two Indian girls in a restaurant sharing a chicken vindaloo and eating it with a fork!

Food plays an important part in Indian social life as a sign of generosity and welcome. Bowls of *nastro* (the most familiar to us is 'Bombay mix') are served to welcome all guests, a practice that has died out in homes and even most traditional restaurants outside India – such a shame as there are thousands of varieties of *nastro* from corn flakes mixed with lentils and seeds to hard green peas and chick peas dipped in spiced batter then baked.

Indian mothers always want to feed you and every household stocks a few different types of 'nastro' – usually fried snacks, nuts and lentils ready to pour into dishes if guests drop in. I am non-traditional in most senses of the word but even I keep some on the shelves.

The average daily dinner would consist of a vegetable *sabji* or *shak*; a curry type dish made with a very basic sauce with a vegetable added to it. This could be any vegetable but peas, potatoes, lentils or mushrooms are favourites, as well as spinach and cauliflower. It is eaten with freshly rolled, cooked and puffed up *chapattis*. These *chapattis* are just flour and water so are very healthy. They are mixed and cooked simply over a gas flame or in a dry pan.

The *shak* may be followed by *dhal* and basmati rice. Like the Chinese, Indians traditionally eat rice dishes at the end of the meal to fill their stomachs. Sometimes, on the side, there is *raita* (a yogurt-type dip), a *popadom*, a small salad, onions, pickles, and chutneys; to drink there will usually be a salty *lassi* or just water. Desserts are usually fruit or rice-based and are not served immediately after the meal. A few *masala* teas or mint infusions may be enjoyed first, then the sweets are brought out. At the very end of the meal the hostess makes a gesture by offering each of her guests *pan* – a variety of spices and nuts wrapped in a betel leaf. This is an important part of the dining ceremony signifying the end of the feast.

There is a preconception that women eat last in Indian culture because of their inferior position in society but I have been assured this is not a matter of sexism but of practicality. Meals are very often large family affairs cooked and served to numerous guests who eat either sitting on cushions on the floor, on sofas or, nowadays, round a dinner table. The practicality of having extended families and so many guests means that they are not all going to fit in one room at the same time. Because the food is accompanied by a constant supply of freshly rolled and puffed chapattis someone has to stay in the kitchen to keep these coming and the cook of the house, admittedly usually a woman, will therefore keep cooking while others eat.

It makes more sense for the men to eat first along with the children, who would otherwise be moaning about being hungry; then when they are out of the way the women relax and eat together.

There aren't many rules to observe when at the table, or seated around the dishes on the floor. You eat with your right hand as the left hand is considered unclean and must therefore never be used to pick up food. A piece of bread – *chapatti*, *naan* or *papad* – is used to scoop and soak up the sauces and brought to the mouth with the tips of your four fingers and the thumb used to transfer it to your mouth.

You can taste more when you eat with your hands; you also eat smaller mouthfuls so your palate can sense all the different layers of flavour and the subtleties of the spices.

Although dishes are often served all at once, when eating a *thali* (a complete meal served on a single platter comprising a couple of small portions of *shak*, *dhal*, pickle, yogurt, rice and *chapatti*) it is considered important to eat each dish in turn, separately. The reason for this rule is simply to aid digestion and to ensure that the taste buds can appreciate the flavours of each individual dish.

Even if you don't adhere to the rules completely you should try to eat the dhal and rice last.

Beer is one of the most common choices to accompany Indian food in restaurants across Britain; brands such as Kingfisher, Cobra and Singh are extremely popular. If you prefer to stick to wine to accompany Indian food the most popular choices of white wines are sweet Alsace or an oaky Chardonnay. For red, choose a fruity Cabernet Sauvignon, a light Rioja or even a Barolo. To be more authentic you would not have alcohol but a *lassi* or a freshly squeezed lime soda.

Whatever the dish or drink, stick to the principles of good diet and try to eat the food the way it has been enjoyed in homes for generations and you will develop an appreciation of it far beyond your expectations.

Recipes

Garam Masala
Hot Curry Powder

Bhaftad
Spiced Lamb Cutlets

Masoor Dhal
Red Lentil Curry

Muttar Paneer
Pea and Paneer Curry

Channa Masala
Chick Peas in Masala Curry

Chapatti
Indian Flat Bread

Monkfish Korma
Monkfish in Coconut Sauce

Poso Gujarati
Gujarati Green Beans

Dungri Fudinif Raita
Onion and Mint Raita

Aam Lassi
Mango Lassi

Gulab Jamun
Sweet Sponge Balls in Rose Honey Syrup

Garam Masala
Hot Curry Powder

There isn't just one recipe for curry powder; Indian cooks have their own, often secret, recipes blending as few as three or as many as fifteen different spices and herbs. *Garam* simply means hot and *masala* is the word for a powder blend; so this recipe is for hot curry blend. The word *kari* means pepper is some dialects so this is perhaps where the word curry came from. The first *kari* powder would have been made with pepper and mustard seeds, once the only common spice in India. *Kari* has been available abroad for longer than you might expect.

It was first sold commercially in England as early as 1770 and since then companies have brought out a huge variety of blends, each subtly distinct in flavour and heat.

It is best to make only a small quantity of powder at once as the fresher the mix the better the flavours. This also gives you the chance to adapt your recipe, experimenting with quantities until you find a blend you really enjoy.

3 tbsp coriander seeds	1 tbsp fenugreek seeds
2 tbsp cumin	1 tbsp mustard seeds
1 tbsp turmeric	2 black peppercorns
1 tbsp allspice	1 tbsp chilli powder

PREP:

1 Place all the spices in a pestle and mortar or coffee grinder and blend together

2 Store in a dry airtight container until needed

Channa Masala
Chick Peas in Masala Curry

Any vegetarian diet will look for an alternative source of protein. Chick peas provide this while being tasty, robust and versatile. This is a simple dish to make and is deliciously wholesome and comforting. It is a classic north Indian dish eaten with *roti* or *bhatura* (fried bread) as part of the main meal or a *thali*. It is sometimes eaten mid afternoon as a form of *chaat* mixed with tamarind chutney and served with a *samosa*. Chick peas are superb flavour carriers so you can make your *masala* as mild or as spicy as you like by adding green chillies.

500g tinned or pre–soaked chick peas	4 cloves
1 onion	1 tsp ground cinnamon
2cm ginger	½ tsp ground coriander
2 cloves of garlic	½ tsp *garam masala*
2 glugs of oil	Salt
1 tsp cumin seeds	Water
2 bay leaves	A handful of fresh coriander
2 black cardamom pods	

PREP:

1 Chop onion, ginger and garlic

2 Take a tablespoon of chick peas and crush with a fork; this will be used to thicken the sauce later

3 Chop the coriander leaving a few leaves for garnish

COOK:

1. Heat the oil in a pan and fry the spices until aromatic

2. Add the chopped onion, garlic and ginger

3. Add the whole chick peas, a few tablespoons of water at a time to create a sauce

4. Gently simmer for 10 minutes until the chick peas have softened a little and taken on the spices. Season to taste

5. Stir in the crushed chick peas to create a thick, spicy sauce

6. Stir through the chopped coriander, garnish with the remaining leaves and serve

Bhaftad
Spiced Lamb Cutlets

Northern Indian regional cuisine, such as Kashmiri, favours the use of lamb and mutton in its dishes. Nomads introduced the animals to the mountainous regions centuries ago and they have never left. Spices are used to preserve and tenderise the sometimes tough meat, and most important today to season it. Lamb or mutton is the most popular meat for Muslims and is eaten in abundance to celebrate festivities such as Eid.

I like this dish because it makes a change from wetter curry. The meat is tenderised and seasoned with the cooked spices to they release the maximum amount of flavour into it before the main cooking begins. I mention keeping the same pan after cooking the spices while the meat marinates as there will be flavours and oil left on it and it is a complete waste to wash these away and start from scratch.

2 medium onions	1 tsp cayenne pepper
7cm ginger	2 tomatoes
4 cloves of garlic	4 large lamb cutlets
1 tbsp coriander seeds	Generous glug of oil
1 tbsp brown mustard seeds	Large knob of butter
1 tbsp cumin seeds	1/2 lemon
1/2 tsp ground turmeric	

PREP:

1 Place in a blender the roughly chopped onions, peeled ginger and garlic. Add approximately 50ml water gradually in order to create a thick paste

2 In a pestle and mortar grind the coriander, mustard and cumin seeds with the turmeric and cayenne pepper

3 Blanch, skin, deseed and chop the tomatoes

COOK:

1. In a large frying pan heat the oil and the butter, add the spices and heat until fragrant

2. Allow to cool a little and spread over the lamb cutlets. Allow to marinate for at least 30 minutes

3. In the same pan heat a little more oil and gently fry the onion, garlic, ginger blend

4. Add the tomatoes and lemon juice, stirring to create a thick sauce

5. Turn the heat down to medium and add the lamb cutlets, coating them completely with the paste

6. Cook for just 8-10 minutes spooning over the sauce to flavour the 'crust' of the lamb but leave the centre pure, natural and beautifully pink. If you prefer your lamb tender and cooked through then it is best to add 100ml water, reduce the heat to a simmer, cover and cook for 45 minutes or until the lamb tears easily with a fork

7. Serve on a bed of rice

Masoor Dhal
Red Lentil Curry

Dhal is a staple on most Indian dinner tables, cooked and eaten almost daily by rich and poor, vegetarians and non vegetarians alike. The dhal can be made as a soup or a thicker curry style dish and can be fragrant or pungent depending on the amount of chilli and mustard used.

This recipe is medium hot but well balanced with the more fragrant spices like fenugreek and cinnamon. Split lentils can be cooked without soaking but soaking speeds up the cooking process.

100g split red lentils	1 tsp fenugreek
2cm fresh ginger	2 cinnamon sticks
1 clove of garlic	3 cloves
2 green chillies	$\frac{1}{2}$ tsp turmeric
10 ripe tomatoes (or 2 tins chopped tomatoes)	*Garam masala*
A splash of oil	Salt to taste
	Sugar to taste
1 tsp mustard seeds	$\frac{1}{2}$ lemon

PREP:

1 Soak some red lentils in warm water for about 20 minutes. Once soft, part liquidise half of them and leave to one side

2 Peel and finely chop the ginger and garlic

3 Chop chillies, deseeding to taste

4 Blanch, skin, and squeeze out most of the water and seeds in the tomatoes, then chop

COOK:

1. Coat the base of a saucepan with the oil

2. Add the mustard seeds and fenugreek, cinnamon sticks and cloves. Heat until they crackle, add the turmeric and *garam masala*, then the ginger, chillies and garlic, and fry until soft and golden

3. Add the liquidised lentils and whole lentils and stir, cooking through for a couple of minutes

4. Mix in the freshly chopped tomatoes or tinned tomatoes, add salt and a little sugar to taste, and lastly a few drops of lemon juice

5. Simmer for 20-25 minutes, stirring occasionally, and adjust seasoning

In my house dhal is eaten with rice at the end of the meal as a filler.

Muttar Paneer [Pea and Paneer Curry]

Muttar Paneer
Pea and Paneer Curry

Vegetarian cuisine reigns supreme in India and the diversity of dishes is outstanding. This is a traditional Punjabi dish and typically has a rich gravy sauce over simple ingredients of peas and cheese. *Paneer* is a special Indian cottage cheese that comes in a solid block. It is used in many Indian dishes in the same way as chicken. You can find it in some supermarkets and most Indian grocers and delicatessens packed in pale milky water to keep it moist. Unlike Italian *mozzarella* this cheese does not melt when cooked and unlike Greek *haloumi* it is not too strong or salty. It has been compared to *tofu* but I find it carries flavours much better and browns more easily.

Paneer makes an excellent base ingredient for many vegetarian dishes.

1 green chilli	1 tin chopped tomatoes
1 large onion	4 tbsp tomato purée
2 cloves garlic	100g peas
2cm ginger	Oil for frying
1 block paneer (300g)	Salt and pepper
1 tsp *garam masala*	Few tbsp water
1/2 tsp turmeric powder	
2 tsp *dhana jeera* (ground coriander and cumin seeds; it can be bought ready made from any Indian deli)	

PREP:

1 Finely chop the green chilli, onion, garlic, and ginger

2 Cube the paneer

COOK:

1. Heat some oil in a pan and toss in the cubes of *paneer*. Once they are golden brown on the outside, drain on kitchen paper and set aside

2. Add a small amount of *garam masala*, the *dhana jeera* and a little turmeric powder to the remaining hot oil

3. When fragrant, add the onion and fry for a couple of minutes. Then add the green chilli, garlic and ginger

4. Add the chopped tomatoes and tomato purée. Mix together and season with salt and a little black pepper

5. Add peas, the fried *paneer* and a few tablespoons of water

6. Cover and simmer on a low heat for 20 minutes or until the sauce thickens and soaks through the soft *paneer*

7. Serve on a bed of rice or with *naan* bread

Chapatti
Indian Flat Bread

Chapatti is a type of *roti* or Indian unleavened bread. Freshly rolled, cooked and puffed up *chapattis* accompany curry and *dhal* across India but are native to the north where more wheat than rice is grown. Diners use their left hand to tear off a piece of *chapatti* and wrap it round a morsel of curry soaking up a little of the sauce before popping it into their mouths. There is no fat in *chapattis* so they are extremely healthy although some people like to brush them with ghee once they are puffed up. They are easy to make and are heated directly over the gas flame or on a hot stone called a *tava* or *tawa*. If you are worried about your fingers you can use tongs to hold them, or cook them in a dry frying pan over high heat.

100g plain flour	100ml water
70g whole wheat flour	Pinch of salt

PREP:

1 Make a well with the sifted flour on a clean surface or in a bowl if you prefer

2 Pour the water in gradually and blend with your fingers bringing in a little of the flour each time to create a soft, smooth dough that should not stick to your fingers

3 Cover with a damp cloth and allow to rest for 20 minutes

4 Pinch off a golf-ball sized chunk of dough. Use your hands to squash the ball into a round shape, then roll out on a lightly floured surface turning the dough after each roll so that it stays round and is just a few mm thick

COOK:

1. Hold over a high gas flame or cook in a hot dry frying pan until brown and puffed up

Monkfish Korma
Monkfish in Coconut Sauce

Goa is famous for its fabulous fish and seafood served with the two other staples of the region, coconut and rice. If you travel along the coast the beaches are lined with colourful fishing huts. Coconut palm leaves lie on the sand that glistens with the silver fish drying in the sun. Goan cuisine today is a blend of local, Arabic and Portuguese cooking. The blend of richness and simplicity is captured by this combination of fresh fish and lush coconut sauce. The local chilli is red rather than the usual green and can be used fresh or dry. In this dish dry chillies are used for extra punch on the palate.

Hoki, cod or hake would be good alternatives as they have a firm texture and hold together under the heat.

3 medium onions	3 curry leaves
2cm ginger	3 tbsp turmeric
1 large clove of garlic	4 tbsp chilli powder
500g monk fish tails (or hoki, cod, or hake)	2 tomatoes
	1 can coconut milk
3 tbsp vegetable oil	1 tsp tamarind paste
1 tsp mustard seeds	Juice of $\frac{1}{2}$ a lime
1 tsp fenugreek	
2 dried red chillis	

PREP:

1 Finely chop onions, grate ginger and crush garlic

2 Fillet and cut the fish into large pieces

COOK:

1. Heat the oil and fry mustard seeds and fenugreek until the aromas hit you and you can hear them pop

2. Add the chilli and stir fry for a minute

3. Next add the finely chopped onions, allowing them to soften and caramelize

4. Add the curry leaves, turmeric, chilli powder and toss so that the onions are completely covered

5. Stir in the tomatoes and cook for about 3 minutes

6. Pour in the coconut milk, stir through the tamarind paste, then season to taste

7. Gently place the fish in the sauce and simmer for 5-8 minutes. The fish will cook lightly and retain its moisture taking on the delicate flavours of the sauce without being overpowered

8. Squeeze fresh lime juice over it just before serving

Poso Gujarati [Gujarati Green Beans]

Poso Gujarati
Gujarati Green Beans

Gujarati cooking is almost completely vegetarian; the variety and imagination of its vegetarian dishes are unparalleled in the West. The *thali*, a Gujarati speciality, offers an endless variety of savoury vegetables along with *dhal*, a *shak* and perhaps some sweetmeats. These green beans are a great addition to the *thali* but are equally good served as an accompaniment to richer meat dishes such as lamb *bhaftad*.

1 large onion	½ tsp turmeric powder
4 green chillies	2 tbsp water
400g french beans	2 tbsp dried coconut (optional)
2 large glugs of oil	Salt and pepper
1 tsp mustard seeds	Squeeze of lemon juice
3-4 curry leaves	
2cm ginger	

PREP:

1 Finely chop the onion and chillies

2 Wash and top and tail the French beans

COOK:

1. Heat the oil in a heavy-bottomed pan on medium heat, add the mustard seeds and shake the pan until they begin to pop

2. Add the curry leaves, chopped green chillies and ginger. Sauté lightly, moving the pan constantly, for 1 minute

3. Throw in the chopped onions and fry on medium heat for about 2 minutes

4. Add the beans and turmeric, and season generously with salt

5. Spoon in the water, cover and reduce the heat to a minimum to allow the beans to infuse and steam for about 6-8 minutes or until they are cooked but firm

6. Adjust seasoning, add a squeeze of lemon juice, sprinkle the coconut over them and serve

Dungri Fudinif Raita
Onion and Mint Raita

Raitas are yogurt or curd flavoured with any combination of vegetables, fruits, seeds or herbs. The *raita* balances the meal, the fresh yogurt acting to calm the palate and stomach after the hot spices. It should therefore be eaten at the end of the meal. Most non-Indians tend to eat it at the beginning of the meal on their poppadoms, alongside mango chutney and lime pickle, which works well. Like Greek *tzatziki* it can be eaten with Mexican tortilla chips, but this is, of course, totally unauthentic.

2 fresh mint leaves	½ tsp cumin seeds
1 small onion	Salt and black pepper
200ml natural yogurt	

PREP:

1 Wash and chop the mint. This is done by laying the leaves together, rolling them a little, and chopping into fine strips

2 Peel and finely dice the onion

COOK:

1. Toast the cumin seeds in a dry pan to release their aroma. Allow to cool

2. Mix all the ingredients together and season to taste

3. Keep refrigerated until ready to serve

Aam Lassi
Mango Lassi

This *lassi* is easier on a western palate than the traditional salty *lassi* and is deliciously refreshing and healthy at any time of day. Indians often drink *lassi* with their meals to balance the heat of the spices used. You may already have realised how useless it is to drink water when your mouth is on fire from a spoonful of hot curry, so reach for the *lassi*. the natural fats in the yogurt and milk stop the burn in seconds.

2 ripe mangoes	1 tbsp sugar
300ml plain yogurt	1 tsp rosewater or cardamom powder (optional)
100ml milk	

PREP:

1 Peel, stone and roughly chop the mangoes

2 Blend all the ingredients in a blender – fruit first, then yogurt, rosewater or cardamom powder, and finally milk and sugar. Serve with or without ice

Gulab Jamun [Sweet Sponge Balls in Rose Honey Syrup]

Gulab Jamun
Sweet Sponge Balls in Rose Honey Syrup

Bengali's greatest addition to Indian cuisine is the outstanding spectrum of sweets made from milk: *rasgullas*, *gulab jamuns*, *rasmalai*, and many more. *Gulab jamun* is often served for *Divali*. *Khova* – basically milk reduced to powder, a typically Indian ingredient that was developed to help storage in hot climates – is easy to find although it is not something we use much these days.

The colour of the *gulab jamun* comes from caramelising the lactose in the dish. It can be served, as I have suggested, with a warm honey sauce flavoured with a few drops of a fragrant essence: either rose syrup or vanilla syrup would be delicious with these rich doughy balls but you could also try essence of orange or lemon. A drizzle of cream cuts the sweetness.

The whole dish should be made in advance to allow the balls to soak up all the honey and expand, making it perfect for entertaining. The balls can be stored for up to 5 days in the fridge and all you need do at the last minute is warm the syrup.

195g *khova* (dried evaporated milk)	400g sugar
1½ tbsp self-raising flour	2 tbsp runny honey
50ml milk, as needed	15ml rose water or 1 tsp rose essence
1 tsp ghee or unsalted butter	200ml ghee for deep frying
600ml water	

PREP:

1 Mix milk powder and flour in a bowl

2 Warm the milk and melt in it a teaspoon of butter or ghee

3 Sprinkle the milk mixture gradually into the bowl working it in with the flour until you have a soft, pliable dough

4 Oil your hands and pinch off approximately 20 large walnut-sized portions of the dough, and roll them into balls, making sure you roll out as many of the cracks in the dough as possible. Place the balls on an oiled plate

5 Make the syrup by mixing the water, honey and sugar in a pan over a moderate heat. Stir until the sugar has dissolved. Boil for five minutes, remove the pan from the heat. Stir in the rose water or essence and set aside

COOK:

1. When the ghee for frying has been heated to a moderate temperature, slide in the balls, one by one. Don't move them at first, just let them sink and turn the pan from side to side to keep them from sticking to the bottom or to each other

2. The balls should float after about 3 minutes. Use a spoon to keep them moving and turn them until they are evenly browned

3. Test one ball by draining off as much of the excess oil as possible with kitchen paper and putting it into the rose syrup. If it swells but stays firm then it is done, and you can proceed with the rest

4. Allow the balls to soak in the syrup for an hour or so, then gently warm through before serving

A Malaysian Kitchen

Introduction to Malaysian Cuisine

Trade winds blow to and from China, the Arabian Gulf and India with Malaysia at their centre. It was trade that created the country and trade that forms its backbone and the essence of its cuisine, today as in centuries past.

It is speculated that Arabian traders brought pasta noodles to Indonesia and the Malay Peninsula, possibly as early as the thirteenth century. In the early 1400s, the Chinese Admiral Zheng led the way for large-scale international exploration and trade, setting sail on junks manned by more than 25,000 men. The seamen brought with them wok-cooking methods, herbs and spices and, of course, chopsticks. By the 1600s the Chinese had established trading routes all along the west coast of the Malay Peninsula and settlements followed. At this time only men were allowed to travel on the trading ships so when they came ashore they took local brides. The offspring of these unions were known as *Nyonyas* for girls and *Babas* for boys.

The Malaccan Straits born people became known as *Peranakans*. With its birth in these bonds, Nyonya cuisine is sometimes called *makanan embok-embok* or 'the food of love'. The Straits people have remained very distinct; the Nyonya women especially retaining their own code of dress and decoration as well as a now renowned cuisine. Recipes are closely guarded secrets passed only from mother to daughter. The meticulous preparation of herbs and spices to make the basis of each dish was, and still is, a source of great pride and mothers teach their daughters how to grind these exceptional pastes from a very early age.

Aesthetics are of great importance, something clearly evident in their food, its presentation and the ornate crockery used. All are colourful, delicate and beautiful.

The Chinese were, of course, not the only traders to come to this region. Because of the excellent conditions and protected waters of the Straits, many European vessels in search of shelter were drawn in too. The Portuguese set up the earliest European settlement. They were followed by the Dutch and finally the British, who established the monumental British East India Trading Company. Modern Malaysia was formed in 1963 through a merging of Malaya, Singapore, and the island states of Sabah and Sarawak. Again the union of these different peoples, although not always harmonious, brought a culinary union of ingredients and cooking methods.

Regional variations are still evident in Malaysian cuisine. In Penang, for example, sourness dominates the foods, perhaps because of its proximity to Thailand. Dishes are characterized by chilli, lime and tamarind, whilst food from Kedah state is prepared using more Indian spices, an abundance of coconut milk, coriander and cumin. This is because Kedah was the first stopping point for Indian traders from the West. There is also a more pronounced Arab influence there than in Malacca, which was more heavily influenced by the Chinese because it was more accessible from the East.

Whatever the herb or spice, the region or the ethnic group, Malaysian cuisine and much of its culture can be summed up by an overriding sense of harmonious union. The harmonious union of peoples throughout time, of different cultures within one nation, of different religions, dress and language and, of course, the harmonious union of flavours, cooking styles and ingredients to make a truly exceptional cuisine. Malaysia can truly be seen as a melting pot of the East.

Flavours of a Malaysian Kitchen

The prevailing characteristics of Malaysian food are tangy, spicy, aromatic and flavourful dishes that incorporate a variety of fresh herbs, pungent roots such as *galangal* and turmeric, pounded with dried spices.

Malaysian cuisine probably uses more aromatic leaves than any other. The delicate *pandanus* leaf, also known as screwpine, is used for both colour and aroma. Banana leaves, not aluminium foil, are used in grilling to really bring out the flavours of the meat and fish. Kaffir lime leaves are used in spicy gravies as are Malaysian *laksa* leaves. Their curry leaves are smaller and stronger than their Indian counterparts.

Candlenuts (the same size and shape as macadamias) are used for both flavour and texture. *Belacan* — a strong dried shrimp paste — is used universally to give the food characteristic fragrance and depth. It is of Nyonya origin (from Malaka) and from there it has spread to other states. It is always combined with chilli and used in conjunction with many other ingredients.

Fresh seasonings and dried spices are pounded together by hand in a mortar and pestle with a little oil to make a *rempah* — literally an 'augmentation of spices' — with different blends for meat, chicken, fish, seafood and vegetables. It is a common misconception that *rempah* is always hot and spicy: what is important is its fragrance, not that it is chilli hot. This can be achieved by using the freshest ingredients and frying the spices before adding the liquid in the form of coconut milk or tamarind juice. The use of a mortar and pestle is still considered superior to a food processor as shredding along 'natural lines' brings out greater aroma and intensity. Finding a rhythm is the key to success, since this will result in more consistency. It is said that a Nyonya can determine the culinary skill of a new daughter-in-law simply by listening to her preparing *rempah* in a mortar. If she is attentive, patient and delicate with the herbs and spices she will act in the same way with her husband and his family.

Malaysian cooks use light soy sauce and sugar to balance their dishes in addition to salt and pepper. The preferred sugar, especially in Nyonya cooking, is palm sugar known as *gula malaka* a dense dark root that can be bought whole or as a syrup.

Pork rarely finds its way into commercially available Malaysian cuisine for religious reasons but it is often a favoured meat in Chinese and Nyonya cuisine. Malay cuisine uses a lot of beef but Indian cuisine in Malaysia avoids beef because of religious beliefs, using lamb and mutton instead. The long coastline and established fishing industry make seafood very popular.

The central component to most Malaysian meals is rice. Other than grain rice, local pancakes known as *roti* are an accompaniment to most spicy 'gravies' e.g. *roti jala*, *roti canai*, *thosai*, *chapatti*, etc. A variety of noodles are also used: thick, thin, 'rat's tails' rice noodles, egg noodles, and mung bean noodles (known as 'glass' noodles) are used for many soups and spicy dishes.

Coconut milk and freshly grated coconut feature in many Malaysian dishes, especially desserts. One of the main tools in a traditional Malaysian kitchen is a coconut grater. In view of the distinct lack of fresh coconuts in the UK there is no call for one here but a good Malaysian cook would sneer at desiccated or dried coconut in the same way an English chef might look at gravy granules.

Although the importation of Malaysian tropical fruits and vegetables allows us to enjoy such delicacies as

rambutan, mangosteens, starfruit, papaya and guava, there is one fruit that has never been adopted in the West and is unlikely to become popular. The durian fruit is notoriously smelly and has thick, spiky thorns on its heavy green shell. The flesh is so pungent that it is banned from hotels and shopping malls. To enjoy it you must suspend your sense of smell and taste the soft, creamy, delicate, white flesh for a burst of sweet sherbet-like fruit. Like many other Malaysian delicacies, it is unique and must be eaten to be appreciated.

Contents of a Malaysian Store Cupboard

Chilli – dried, fresh, powder
Cloves
Coriander – leaves, roots, powder
Cumin
Cinnamon
Cardamom
Garlic
Ginger – young, old
Galangal
Lemon Grass
Onions
Shallots
Star Anise
Tamarind

Turmeric – roots and leaves
Candlenuts
Gula Malaka (Palm Sugar)
Sesame Oil
Soy Sauce – light and dark
Kicap manis/Tim cheong Sweet
Soy Sauce
Rice Vinegar
Rice Wine
Chicken Stock
Udang kering (Dried Prawns)
Belacan (Dried Shrimp Paste)
Heh koh (Dried Prawn Paste)
Tofu (up to 30 varieties)
Rice: fragrant, glutinous, long grain,
black, brown

Noodles: rice, 'glass', wheat, egg
Tapioca

Coconut Milk and Cream
Grated Coconut
or Desiccated Coconut
Taucheo (Salted Soy Beans)
Spring Onion
Bean Sprouts
Bamboo Shoots
Dried Chinese Mushrooms
Ikan bilis (Dried Whitebait)
Pickled Vegetables, e.g. *Kiam chai*
(Pickled Mustard Greens)
Exotic fruits: Lychees, Rambutan,
Starfruit

Pandanus Leaves
Kaffir Lime Leaves
Banana Leaves
Curry Leaves

Lessons learnt along the way...

Malaysian food is as varied as the people who created it. Its overriding feature is its abundance. Malaysians eat some five meals a day: breakfast is the most important and should never be skipped; traditionally there is a break for tea at ten followed by a snack at eleven; lunch is at noon followed by a mid-afternoon sweet snack; dinner is served in the early evening but supper can be as late as three in the morning:

For breakfast my parents have Nasi Lemak, coconut rice, preferably served on a banana leaf with small portions of a variety of curries or sambal, egg and cucumber. It smells of coconut and is rich but fragrant rather than sweet. Or they have Lontong, essentially clear glass noodles in a coconut-based soup. It is not chilli hot, but has lots of turmeric and herbs in it. It has vegetables too. We would also have little rice cakes with vegetables and meat.

Malaysians follow the eastern belief that eating 'cooling' food – clear soups, served hot or cold, bean curd/tofu-based products and leafy green vegetables – on a hot day keeps you cool. Clear coloured fruit such as mangosteens and lychees are considered 'cooling'. They counteract the 'heatiness' of opaque, heavy fruits like durian. 'Heaty' foods – including chillies, curries, fried food and red meat – are eaten in moderation. Spices make it harder to eat a lot: the more spices in the food the less your stomach can take, so although Malaysians eat often, they do not eat large amounts, which helps them retain their petite figures – all together better in a hot climate. Of course these rules do not apply in Britain:

New generations, like me, are becoming more health conscious because of the change in lifestyle so we try to make things lighter than before and cut down on the carbohydrate and fat, adapting the cuisine to make it a

healthier option. It is a reasonable success. Eating little and often is also growing in popularity over here.

Because we eat so often we are really relaxed about food.

Traditional Malaysians eat with their hands from a banana leaf or the plate. They used to say that food tasted better when you feel it with your fingertips (except in the case of a particularly soupy meal). Today a knife, fork and spoon are as common as chopsticks.

It is a real art form; you use only the tips of the fingers and thumb of your right hand and scoop the food, cleanly and neatly forming bulbouses, which you pop into your mouth using your thumb. Your palm never gets dirty. Definitely something you have to practise. Some women are so good they don't even smudge their lipstick. I was rubbish when I started because we didn't do it at home but when I used to visit my friends at their houses I had a chance to practise. In Malaysian restaurants some people still use their hands. They used to bring bowls of fragrant water to the table so that you could wash your fingers afterwards.

Eating is a communal activity whether at home or in a restaurant. Families and friends eat together whenever possible. The head of the table, usually the head of the family, is in charge.

As a child you never start a meal without inviting the elders to eat first. You would say "Baba, Mama please eat". Then, with a nod, it's every man for himself. All the dishes are laid out at once and you help yourself. Slurping is considered good manners because it shows you are enjoying your food.

Because Malaysians are descendants of Malays, Indians, Chinese and Westerners there are many religious beliefs. This has led to a diverse and flexible use of ingredients in traditional dishes. Instead of pork, duck might be used; in place of beef, chicken; and instead of any meat, one of the many varieties of tofu.

As with most cultures, food plays an important part in celebrations. With so many religions, feasts are frequent. At Chinese New Year families sit down for a steamboat; *rendang* and *serunding* are a must for Eid; and *muruku*, also known as Bombay mix for Diwali. Sweets are an important part of all celebrations. Nowadays it is not unusual to have an amalgamation of all the different cuisines at any of these celebrations.

Although some dishes are eaten to mark certain celebrations they are by no means restricted to those times. Food is not seen as something that should be reserved for special occasions or special guests. Malaysians share the best of everything they have, every day, with their family and friends round the dinner table. Dishes served at home almost every day are no different from those served for celebrations or those that would be offered to royalty.

In fact, the best cuisine in Malaysia is associated with home cooking rather than restaurant cooking because

each family takes pride in the fact that its secret recipe is the best. For example, the complex techniques associated with certain Nyonya dishes are handed down from one generation to the next, although not always from mother to daughter in the traditional way:

My mother very rarely cooked. She did not have the time because of the work and therefore it was done by the maid. Grannies usually teach the maids to cook so the family recipes carry on. Growing up I spent a lot of time with the maid keeping out of trouble, so I would watch what she did and she would get me to help prepare food by plucking a chicken or cleaning a squid. It was almost like 'playtime'. I think you pick up skills without realising it.

Recipes

Kiam Chai
Duck and Preserved Cabbage Soup

Sambal Udang Kering
Seasoned Minced Dried Prawns

Satay Ayam Babi
Chicken and Pork Satay Skewers

Ngoh Hiang
Five Spice Meat Rolls

Popiah
Pancakes filled with Mixed Meat,
Vegetables and Garnishes

Gulai Udang
King Prawns in Mild Curry Sauce

Laksa Lemak
Mixed Meat, Shrimp, Tofu, Vegetables,
and Rice Noodles with Curry Gravy

Nasi Lemak
Coconut Rice with Sambal and Mixed Condiments

Ikan Asam Surani
Sea Bass in Tamarind and Turmeric Gravy

Serunding
Beef with Spiced Coconut

Sambal Belacan
Prawn Chilli Sauce

Sago Gula Malaka
Sago Pudding with Palm Sugar

Kaya
Egg Jam

Kiam Chai
Duck and Preserved Cabbage Soup

Although they have an abundance of fresh vegetables the Teochew used loads of preserved vegetables, especially in soups. They are really delicious and because they are preserved in salt you can omit the soy or salt in cooking and the stock base tastes richer. The Teochew love pork and also use a lot of duck in their cooking but this does result in a slightly oily soup. If you want to make it lighter remove the skin from the duck or replace it with lean pork or chicken. Malaysians would leave the duck pieces whole but I think it is really tricky to eat soup with large bones in and have not mastered the art of chewing the meat off bones politely so I recommend you strip the meat off the bones and return it to the soup before serving.

300g preserved/salted mustard greens (or 1 white cabbage and 100g salt in 1 litre of water)	300g pork spare ribs
	1 tomato
	2 litres water
2cm ginger root	Salt
1 tamarind pod or 1 tsp tamarind paste	1 tbsp rice wine
½ duck, chopped in pieces	

PREP:

1 If you don't have salted mustard greens you can make your own by chopping a cabbage in large chunks and putting it into a bowl with the salt water mix and leaving it overnight or longer. Otherwise, simply rinse your salted cabbage a few times

2 Peel and bruise the ginger

3 Deseed the tamarind pod

4 Cut the duck and pork into large pieces leaving any bones in

COOK:

1. Place the pork in the cold water in a pan and bring to the boil, skimming off any fat

2. Add the duck and boil again, skimming off any impurities or excess fat

3. Add the cabbage, ginger, tamarind, tomato and rice wine

4. Simmer for 30 minutes until the duck is tender

5. Remove the duck and take the meat off the bone with a fork. Return the large meaty pieces to the soup

6. Season to taste

This is a classic Nyonya dish but my paternal grandmother, who was Teochew, used to make it a lot. It is a favourite for family dinners – simple but wholesome.

Sambal Udang Kering
Seasoned Minced Dried Prawns

Most British Malaysians consider this an essential item in their store cupboard. It is a really tasty topping for rice that is very simple to prepare. It can also be served on hot buttered toast with a few slices of cucumber as an easy snack.

Once prepared it can be refrigerated or frozen.

300g dried prawns	6 red chillies
1 tbsp lime juice	3 tbsp oil
300g shallots	2 tbsp sugar

PREP:

1 Rinse prawns and mix them with the lime juice

2 Peel and slice shallots. Crush chillies into a paste in a pestle and mortar or blender

COOK:

1. Heat the oil in a wok and stir fry the shallots until browned. Drain with a perforated spoon

2. Fry the chilli in the remaining oil

3. Once the oil has turned red, remove from the heat and drain in a sieve. Throw away the pulp and return the oil to the wok

4. Stir fry the prawns in the chilli oil, add the sugar and continue to fry for 4-5 minutes

5. Put back the shallots and toss with the chilli oils

Food in Malaysia is not just a national passion, it is more an obsession. If you are with Malaysians or when travelling the country they are always asking when you ate, where you ate and what you ate. It is not surprising then that they have adopted the Chinese greeting in place of hello that translates as 'Have you eaten yet?'

Satay Ayam Babi
Chicken and Pork Satay Skewers

Cooked over a charcoal fire then dipped in thick peanut sauce, Satay is a traditional celebration food and a favourite for snacking and late suppers after a big night out. If you want to impress your friends prepare them before you go out and pop them under the grill for 10 minutes when you get home. They will love you for it!

	For the dipping sauce:
150g chicken	10 red chillies
150g pork	1 lemon grass stalk
½ stalk lemon grass	3 tbsp oil
5 shallots	2 tbsp tamarind paste
1 tbsp coriander	2 tbsp sugar
½ tsp cumin	300g peanuts
½ tsp turmeric	3cm ginger
½ tsp cinnamon	6 shallots
½ tsp salt	3 cloves of garlic
2 tbsp crushed peanuts	
1 tbsp oil	
20 wooden skewers	
2 cucumbers	

PREP:

• Satay

1 Cut the meat into cubes and tenderise lightly with a rolling pin covered in cling film

2 Chop lemon grass and shallots, blend with spices and peanuts

3 Marinate the meat in this mixture for at least 30 minutes

4 Thread the meat onto satay sticks

• Dipping sauce

1 Soak the chillies in hot water, then deseed and chop roughly

2 Peel and crush white part of lemon grass in a pestle and mortar

3 Roughly chop ginger, shallots and garlic, and blend together

4 Dilute the tamarind paste in 150ml water

5 Put peanuts in a bag and crush roughly with a rolling pin

COOK:

1. In a wok heat oil and stir fry lemon grass, ginger, shallots, chilli and garlic

2. Add tamarind marinate and cook for 2 minutes

3. Add salt, sugar and crushed peanuts

4. Simmer until you have a thick sauce. Set aside to cool

5. Place under a hot grill for 7-10 minutes, turning frequently and basting with the marinate as they cook

6. Meanwhile, slice the cucumber into bite-size chunks and set aside

7. Serve the satay skewers with diced cucumber and the thick dipping sauce

Ngoh Hiang
Five Spice Meat Rolls

These rolls make a good snack or starter dipped in sweet chilli sauce. The bean curd sheets can be bought in packs from most Chinese grocers and some supermarkets. Look for the ones that are oiled and foldable (usually marked on the pack). They are fragile so you will need to moisten them with some water using a pastry brush or damp kitchen towel before you roll each one. Handle them with care as they tear easily. The skins must be rolled tightly round the filling or they may open and absorb the oil. The tighter they are rolled the crisper they will be.

1 pack bean curd sheets	1 tbsp five spice powder
2 spring onions	2 tbsp light soya sauce
300g minced pork, beef or chicken	Splash of sesame oil
	1 egg
1 tbsp flour	Oil for deep frying

PREP:

1 Cut the bean curd sheets into squares just a little bigger than a CD case

2 Chop the spring onions

3 Put meat, onion, sesame oil, soy, five spice powder and flour into a bowl and mix to make the firm, slightly sticky filling

4 Take a sheet of bean curd, put a tablespoon of mixture at one end and roll it up tightly like a spring roll: take the sheet over the filling, tuck it under tightly, roll once, then fold in the sides and roll again as tightly as possible. Repeat to the end.

5 Seal the edge with a little whisked egg

COOK:

1. Deep fry until golden brown

2. Drain on kitchen paper and serve on a platter with sweet chilli dipping sauce

Popiah
Pancakes filled with Mixed Meat, Vegetables and Garnishes

If you love filling Chinese pancakes with duck and plum sauce or piling the chicken into *fajitas* you will love *popiah*. The name comes from the Chinese *po* for 'thin' and *pia* for 'wrapper'. They are to be enjoyed with family and friends: a spread of fillings are laid out on the table with a huge pile of *popiah*. Everyone picks up a *popiah* and helps themselves to the various fillings. The end result is a delicate, combination of textures, flavours, heat and aroma.

Traditionally *pandanus* leaves are placed between the *popiah* so the cook can count them easily and ensure they do not stick together. They also give a delicate fragrance to the *popiah*. If you do not have *pandanus* leaves use strips of foil or baking paper.

5 eggs	2 tbsp oil
Pinch of salt	350ml water
150g flour	

PREP:

1 Crack the eggs into a bowl and beat without whisking too much air into the mixture

2 Add salt and sift in the flour stirring all the time to make a smooth, lump-free batter

3 Add water and oil to thin the batter to a runny consistency that will still coat the back of a spoon

4 Set aside to rest for 20 minutes

COOK:

1. Add a drop of oil to a large flat pan

2. Heat the pan over a low heat and pour a spoonful of batter onto it. Tilt the pan to spread the batter to the edges, creating a circle. The *popiah* should be pale and thin so there is no need to turn or flip them as you would a pancake

3. Peel away from the pan and place on a plate ready for use with the fillings

As kids we would always try to see who could cram the most filling into their wrapper without it falling apart on them as they ate. They are absolutely delicious, fun to share with friends and family, and pretty healthy too.

Popiah Filling

This dish constitutes the main filling served with the *popiah*, the central part of the feast.

1 clove of garlic	500ml chicken stock
200g tin of bamboo shoots	50g soy beans (optional)
1/2 turnip (optional)	Generous splash soy sauce
100g pork tenderloin	1 tsp sugar
75g firm tofu	Large pinch of salt
Handful of small prawns	Oil to stir fry

PREP:

1 Chop garlic

2 Thinly slice bamboo shoots and turnip

3 Slice pork into long thin strips

COOK:

1. Heat oil in a wok and stir fry the chopped garlic, adding soy beans if you wish, and a little water

2. Stir fry the pork and set aside

3. Stir fry the tofu until its edges are crispy

4. Toss in pork and prawns and stir fry for another minute

5. Add chopped bamboo shoots, turnip, soy, sugar and salt

6. Pour the stock over and simmer for 20 minutes until the vegetables are tender and the gravy has reduced

7. Serve in a large bowl alongside any or all of the following fillings:
   Lettuce leaves (to prevent fillings from breaking the *popiah*)
   Fried minced garlic
   Kicap Manis/Tim Cheong sweet soy sauce
   Plum sauce
   Crab meat
   Fried Chinese sausage (available as chicken or pork)
   Cooked king prawns
   Shredded cucumber
   Steamed bean sprouts
   Sautéed cabbage
   Ground roasted peanuts
   Fresh coriander
   Fresh chopped chilli
   Strips of omelette or hard boiled eggs

Gulai Udang [King Prawns in Mild Curry Sauce]

Gulai Udang
King Prawns in Mild Curry Sauce

One of the milder Malay dishes. The king prawns are cooked with fragrant lemon grass, ginger and cumin in a rich coconut milk. You can prepare the *rempah* in advance and even cook the dish through to create the sauce and so all that remains to do at the last minute is to throw in the prawns and blast with heat for five minutes. This might be served with steamed rice, or as one of the dishes for a *popiah* or *nasi lemak*.

3 dried chillies	1 tbsp *belacan* (shrimp paste)
2 fresh large green chillies	3 tbsp oil
5 shallots	400ml coconut milk
1 stalk of lemon grass	1 tbsp tamarind paste
25 cm ginger root	300g king prawns
½ tbsp turmeric	1 tbsp sugar
1 tsp coriander powder	Large pinch of salt
½ tsp cumin	
1 clove of garlic	

PREP:

1 Soak dried chillies in hot water for a couple of minutes then chop

2 Slit fresh chillies and deseed if you prefer a milder taste

3 Peel and slice shallots

4 Peel and bruise the lemon grass and ginger

5 Make the *rempah* by blending dried chillies, turmeric, coriander, cumin, garlic and ginger with the *belacan* in a pestle and mortar

COOK:

1. Heat a wok, add oil, stir fry shallots until caramelised, then add the *rempah* and lemon grass, frying until fragrant

2. Add a splash of coconut milk to loosen the paste and simmer for a minute

3. Add tamarind paste and the remaining coconut milk. Bring to the boil, stirring constantly

4. Add the prawns and chillies, reducing the heat to a simmer. Cook for 5 minutes, adding sugar and salt to taste

Laksa Lemak
Mixed Meat, Shrimp, Tofu, Vegetables, and Rice Noodles with Curry Gravy

Malaysians love to discuss the subtle variations of this dish. Most Malaysian states have their own version of *laksa*. However, two basic styles prevail: *asam laksa*, which is sour tasting and based on tamarind juices, and *laksa lemak* with a milder coconut-milk base. *Laksa* is usually enjoyed with the whole family as the more guests there are the more incentive you have to increase the number of ingredients.

Although the list of ingredients for a *laksa* is rather long, some of the meats or the tofu can be omitted if you don't have them or just don't fancy them. The quantities for the meats and tofu are rough estimates; if you have particularly hungry guests increase them, or decrease them if you want a light supper.

Laksa is actually fairly simple to make and can be prepared and almost entirely plated before anyone arrives for dinner, making it the perfect meal for sharing. All you need do as a final touch is heat the curry 'gravy', which you pour over just before serving. If your guests are very slow eaters, as I am, they will think that they have more food than when they started as the noodles expand more and more the longer they sit in the delicious spiced 'gravy'.

5 shallots	Chilli oil (or 10 chillies to 150ml oil)
2 cloves of garlic	1 tsp *belacan* (shrimp paste)
A handful of candlenuts (or cashew nuts)	2 pak choi
5cm of ginger	1 small bundle of rice vermicelli per person
3 dried chillies	
A pinch of turmeric	100g cooked shredded chicken
A handful of coriander	
1 tbsp tamarind paste	2 stalks of lemon grass

100g cooked shredded pork	3 *laksa* leaves (if available)
100g cooked king prawns	200g fried tofu
1 can coconut milk (400g)	Light soy sauce (or salt)
500ml chicken stock	

PREP:

1 Chop the shallots, garlic, candlenuts, ginger and chillies coarsely

2 Blend or process with turmeric, coriander, tamarind paste and a little of the oil. Then add the *belacan* and blend for a few seconds longer to make the *rempah*

3 Chop the pak choi into quarters

4 In a pan of boiling water blanch the pak choi for about 3 minutes, then drain

5 Drop the rice vermicelli into a bowl of boiling water for 4 minutes, drain, and arrange in serving bowls

6 Arrange the chopped chicken, shredded pork, pak choi and a few king prawns on top of the vermicelli

COOK:

1. Heat the remaining oil in a wok or heavy pan

2. Add the *rempah* and lemon grass and fry over a low heat, stirring constantly until the paste is fragrant

3. Add the coconut milk and chicken stock with the *laksa* leaves and bring to the boil, stirring occasionally

4. Add the tofu and simmer until it is cooked

5. Season to taste with a little soy sauce and sugar

6. When you are ready simply pour the *laksa* 'gravy' over the vermicelli and serve immediately

Nasi Lemak

Coconut Rice with Sambal and Mixed Condiments

If Malaysia were to have a national dish, this would have to be a contender. Simply rice cooked in coconut milk with ginger or lemon grass added for extra fragrance. It is eaten at any time of the day or night: breakfast, elevensees, lunch, tea, dinner, supper, post-partying.

Condiments include fried peanuts, fried prawns, cucumber slices, hardboiled egg or strips of omelette and *sambal* the recipe for which is given on page 167. This recipe is best with glutinous rice to guarantee a sticky but delicious consistency.

350g glutinous or long grain rice	390ml coconut milk
5cm root ginger	2 *pandanus* leaves (optional)
1 tsp salt	

PREP:

1 Rinse the rice twice

2 Peel and finely shred the ginger

3 Tie the *pandanus* leaves into knots

COOK:

1. Put the rice and an equivalent amount of water in a large pan. Add half the coconut milk, the ginger and the *pandanus* leaves

2. Mix ingredients well and bring to the boil

3. Cover and lower the heat to simmer for about 25 minutes until the water has been absorbed and the rice is tender

4. Loosen the rice grains with a fork

5. Remove from the heat and sprinkle the rest of the coconut milk over the rice

6. Stir well, cover the pot again and allow it to stand for 10-15 minutes until the rice has absorbed the rest of the coconut milk and is a little sticky

TIP:
To stop a black circle forming round the yolk of the egg once it has boiled, plunge it immediately into cold water.

Ikan Asam Surani

Sea Bass in Tamarind and Turmeric Gravy

Asam is the Malay name for the tamarind fruit, a key feature of this Nyonya style dish that favours sour tones in seasoning to bring out the freshness of the fish. The heady aroma of the spices combined with the richness of the *belacan* makes this a remarkably flavourful dish on the palate though it is light on the stomach. If sea bass is not available Malaysians use red snapper, hake or hoki.

300g white fish fillets	1 tsp turmeric
6 shallots	3 tbsp tamarind paste
3 cloves garlic	400ml water
½ stalk lemon grass	Oil for frying
3 chillies	2 tbsp sugar
1 tbsp *belacan* (shrimp paste)	Pinch salt

PREP:

1 Rinse then cut fish into large pieces

2 Peel and finely slice shallots and garlic

3 Bruise lemon grass

4 Slice chillies and remove seeds if you prefer less heat

5 Create *rempah* by blending dried shrimp (*belacan*) and turmeric

6 Blend the tamarind with water and marinate the fish in it for at least half an hour

COOK:

1. Heat a wok and add the oil. Stir fry the shallots and garlic. Remove them with a perforated ladle and drain

2. In the same pan stir fry the lemon grass and chillies, remove and drain

3. Again in the same pan add the *rempah* mix and tamarind marinate, keeping the fish aside

4. Bring to the boil and reduce by a quarter

5. Add the fried ingredients, sugar and then the fish

6. Lower the heat and cook for 5-7 minutes. Add salt to taste

Serunding
Beef with Spiced Coconut

This is beef fried with roasted grated coconut that is traditionally cooked for up to twenty hours in order to produce a dried shredded *biltong* like consistency. The combination of flavours works so well together that when cooked quickly it makes a tender, sweet and fragrant dish that is too good to wait for. As it is quite hard to get freshly grated coconut outside of South-East Asia or the Caribbean this recipe has been adapted to use desiccated coconut. Beef and coconut complement each other: the meat is cooked until it is tender and the coconut absorbs the juices while releasing a sweet scent and heady taste.

2 lemon grass stalks	1 tsp tamarind pulp
7cm ginger	3 tbsp palm sugar
1 tsp cumin powder	280ml water
2 tsp coriander powder	Large pinch of salt
1 tsp turmeric	500g desiccated coconut
6 tbsp oil	2 tbsp coconut milk
600g beef	

PREP:

1 Peel and chop the lemon grass and ginger

2 Blend with the cumin, coriander and turmeric to make a *rempah* paste

COOK:

1. Heat the oil in a wok and fry the *rempah* paste

2. Add the beef and brown it well

3. Add the tamarind, palm sugar and salt

4. Mix in a little water to create a sauce so that the meat is completely coated with all the flavours

5. Turn down the heat, add the desiccated coconut and coconut milk and simmer until the meat is tender and the juices have been absorbed

6. Allow the meat to rest for a few minutes before serving over hot white rice

Sambal Belacan [Prawn Chilli Sauce]

Sambal Belacan
Prawn Chilli Sauce

Sambal is a thick, rich chilli sauce that can range from mildly hot to absolutely fiery. There are a number of different *sambals* in Malaysian cuisine all using a variety of peppers, chillies, and other ingredients such as dried prawns, tamarind, candlenuts, or simply salt and pepper. As with many Malaysian dishes the smell of the raw ingredients can seem overwhelming, especially the dried shrimp, but the end result is so much the richer for it.

This *sambal* is excellent served with *nasi lemak* or with grilled fish or chicken.

8 dried chillies	A pinch of salt
4 shallots	1 tsp sugar
1 clove of garlic	1 tsp *ikan bilis* (small dried salted whitebait/anchovies)
1 tsp *belacan* (shrimp paste)	
½ cup tamarind juice	Splash of oil for frying

<u>PREP:</u>

1 Soak dried chillies in hot water

2 Finely dice shallots

3 Chop garlic

4 Pound chillies, garlic, shallots and shrimp paste in a pestle and mortar until you have a smooth thick paste

COOK:

1. Heat the oil in a wok and fry the pounded ingredients until fragrant

2. Add shallots, tamarind juice, salt and sugar

3. Cook until the gravy thickens

4. Add *ikan bilis*, mix well, and pour into a small bowl for guests to spoon over their rice

Sago Gula Malaka
Sago Pudding with Palm Sugar

After the chilli heat of Malaysian food this cooling, silky coconut dessert is perfect. The *gula malaka* makes an intense, sweet syrup but using a couple of teaspoons of coconut milk cuts through it, ensuring a combination that is both refreshing and indulgent.

For the Pudding	For the Syrup
200g pearl sago	330ml water
660ml water	5 tbsp *gula malaka*
1 can coconut cream	3 tbsp white sugar
A handful of desiccated coconut (optional)	2 *pandanus* leaves (if available)

PREP:

1 Wash sago and soak for 5 minutes until swollen. Drain well

2 Pound the *pandanus* leaves in a pestle and mortar and squeeze out the juice

COOK:

1. Bring 600ml water to the boil

2. Add ½ can coconut cream and the sago. Simmer until the sago is soft and transparent

3. Drain and run under the cold water tap to rinse off any excess starch

4. Spoon into serving bowls, pressing down to make it compact, then refrigerate

5. Put in a pan the water, palm sugar, white sugar and the juice of the *pandanus* leaves. Heat until the sugars have dissolved and the syrup coats the back of a spoon. Refrigerate until cool

6. To serve, turn out the bowls of sago onto a plate or into an ice cream glass, pour 2-3 tbsp syrup over each, followed by a splash of coconut cream and a sprinkle of desiccated coconut to garnish

Kaya
Egg Jam

Kaya is one of those products that most Malaysians will have in their fridge. It is a sumptuously rich, thick egg jam that is delicious spread on breads for breakfast or as a sweet treat throughout the day. I tried it on toasted raisin bread and cinnamon bread and found it sublime. The raisins and cinnamon balance the sweetness of the jam, and at the same time bring out the subtle aromas of the coconut.

| 3 eggs | 150g caster sugar |
| 2 egg yolks | 250ml thick coconut milk |

PREP:

1 Break the eggs into a mixing bowl

2 Add egg yolks and beat until well blended and pale yellow

3 Add the sugar stirring continuously until the paste is smooth

4 Slowly add the thick coconut milk and continue to beat until the sugar is fully dissolved and the coconut milk well blended

COOK:

1. Pour into a heavy based pan and heat over a gentle flame, stirring constantly to prevent it crystallising or scrambling, until the sugar caramelises and you have a thick dark jam

2. Pour into a sterilised jar and store in the fridge until you are ready to serve it

An Estonian Kitchen

Introduction to Estonian Cuisine

Five thousand years ago the Estonians left the Urals and chose the eastern shores of the Baltic Sea and the southern coast of the Gulf of Finland as their homeland. This tiny country has had many rulers: since the thirteenth century the Danes, Germans, Swedes and Russians have all left their cultural stamp on the land and its cuisine. Sauerkraut and beetroot as well as horseradish and salted cucumbers feature on most traditional menus. Dining 'Russian style' – in a series of courses rather than from a single display laid out all at once – was practised in Estonia long before its European cousins adopted this protocol.

In 1918 Estonia won independence, establishing the First Estonian Republic, only to be annexed by the Soviet Union in 1940. From being a wealthy, developed nation Estonia slipped into decline. Finally, in 1991, after the collapse of communism the Second Republic was established and Estonia joined the European Union in 1994. Despite massive political changes and dramatic swings of fortune Estonians are as proud of their peasant past as of their prosperous times. Nowhere is this more evident than on the plate.

Two-thirds of the Estonian border is water; there are more than fifteen hundred islands and islets and over fourteen hundred lakes that make up its landscape with the result that it is rich in fish stocks. Fish is commonly smoked or marinated; its best known products are spicy or smoked sprat and marinated herring.

The many forests provide mushrooms, nuts, honey and saps that are made into popular refreshing drinks such as birch juice. Wild herbs such as dill, fennel, mint and parsley grow all over the countryside and feature strongly in the diet.

Because of the cold winters heavy, filling stews, soups and roasts are enjoyed at home and in restaurants all over the country. Fortunately the temperature rises in summer and the land comes to life exploding with an abundance of fresh berries, fruits and vegetables that lighten the diet and draw people out of their relative hibernation.

The flavours of an Estonian Kitchen

Humble Estonian cuisine developed from peasant foods with little emphasis on extravagant flavours or decoration. Seasonings are simple: salt and pepper, whatever fresh herbs are in season, and a few spices, usually in foreign influenced dishes such as paprika in stews, copying their neighbour's goulash.

Most Estonians are committed carnivores with pork traditionally the most popular meat. A very special kind of ham matured in the sauna is one of the carnivores' delights. Because of the Estonians' historic appreciation of natural, organic food and farming methods, game and blood dishes feature heavily in their cuisine. In addition to sausages they eat blood bread, blood pancakes and even blood cake!

You would think that with so much of Estonia being bordered with water, fresh fish would be in abundance on the plate, but Estonians are more likely to cook with salted, smoked, dried or pickled fish than fresh, a habit from more frugal days. They frequently dine on fish that are no longer fashionable in other European countries because of their association with poverty: eels, mackerel, herring and sprats are all common. Tallinn sprats are the most revered of all. Preparing sprats was women's work and folklore has it that these Tallinn sprats were the sweetest anywhere, so good that even aristocratic women would prepare them. I can't imagine the aristocracy of today happy to be seen in the pages of *Hello* magazine packing fish!

Dairy produce is popular in the Estonian diet, but because of traditional storage methods sour milk, buttermilk and curds became more common than fresh milk and cheese. This is still the case today. Most traditional Estonian dairy products come in the form of cottage cheese or curds flavoured with everything from ham or shrimps to jam and chocolate. Estonians are also fond of making soup with milk, both savoury and sweet versions that are served as starters, main courses or desserts.

Cereals play an important part in the Estonian diet with porridge and gruel as staples. There is a cereal borne of its poorest peasant days unique to Estonian cuisine: *kama* is a mixture of rough grain flour and peas. It is often combined with fresh or sour milk and seasoned with salt or sugar. Like porridge it can be thick and creamy, dry and solid, or runny. Estonians also eat *grits*, a roughage that neither sounds nor looks particularly appetising.

Dark breads such as sour rye bread are more common than white or brown wheat breads. There are about thirty types of rye bread, which make superb open sandwiches with layers of smoked fish, gherkins and sour cream contrasting with the black dough.

The vegetables most common in Estonian cuisine are again synonymous with poor man's food: cabbage, carrots, pumpkin, beetroot, turnips and potatoes. They are baked, fried, mashed and pickled to enhance their flavour and diversify their textures and are often served with dill pickle and sour cream to add another dimension. Pickling vegetables and berries to preserve them for the long winter months seems to be the pastime of most Estonian grandmothers, even those who have long left the cold winters behind them. You can expect to see jars of pumpkin and mushrooms, cucumbers with blackberry leaves and dill, as well as loganberry, whortleberry, lingonberry, and the more common cranberry in most family store cupboards.

The average Estonian would also be used to getting fruit from the garden of the family summer house, not the preserve of the wealthy, so even in big cities people are familiar with good organic produce. Apple and rhubarb pies served with lashings of whipped cream are not reserved for a special Sunday treat but would be on the table throughout the year. Berry and mushroom picking in the woods are popular pastimes, the best spots well-kept family secrets.

Fruit and berries are also made into fresh juices. The sap of trees such as the birch are tapped and their sweet nectar made into a surprisingly refreshing drink. Old Estonians used to brew hundreds of litres of beer per household when the festive seasons began. They are still big beer drinkers, preferring it to wine, and have developed many beer and mead drinks from cereals, hops, and honey. As Estonians traditionally take a long holiday over the Christmas period men brewed their beer at home. It would be done on St. Thomas's day and they would make enough to last until Epiphany. They began in the middle of the night "so the evil eye did not spot the brew" but more likely an excuse to get together and drink among friends. The various beers and *viin* (the equivalent of vodka) are among the strongest in Europe and Estonians are not shy when it comes to drinking them. If you learn nothing else, one very important Estonian word is *Terviseks* (cheers).

Since its admission to the European Union the doors have opened on Estonia and its cuisine. Trade with the western world is no longer limited to butter and bacon. We have been invited to enjoy the fruits of the land and learn that the best peasant food can sit comfortably on the dinner tables of aristocrats and the masses alike, although I'm not sure that pickling sprats will catch on.

Contents of an Estonian Store Cupboard

Rye

Oats

Barley

Semolina

Dried Peas and Beans

Potatoes

Cabbage

Sauerkraut

Beetroot

Onions

Mushrooms

Soola Kurgid (Gherkins in Brine)

Jelly

Fish Roe

Sprats

Pike

Pickled Herring

Goose

Pork

Blood Sausage

Buttermilk or Soured Milk

Sour Cream

Cottage Cheese

Quark

Eggs

Smoked Cheese

Smoked Meats

Marzipan

Cranberries

Blackberries

Apples

Lemons

Mustard

Marjoram

Fennel

Bay Leaves

Cloves

Parsley

Dill

Sorrel

Garlic

White Vinegar

Almonds

Honey

Kasemahl (Birch Juice)

Viin (Vodka)

Lessons learnt along the way...

Estonians do not have a long tradition of dining at the table together except for special occasions, perhaps because of relative poverty and demanding agricultural lifestyles. Eating a meal was once considered a sacred ritual. Because of the reverence surrounding food it was not uncommon for people to dine in complete silence. Now the sacred nature of food is reflected in the three tenets of Estonian dining: health, taste, and cost.

Estonians today are actually really relaxed when eating. Everyone sits round the table and you serve yourself from the dishes that are brought out by the cook. First soup, then the main course: fish or meat with vegetables, potatoes and sauce. We don't usually have desserts, only simple dishes. One that my Nana made up was bread soaked in milk with fresh fruit, such as strawberries, and a sprinkling of sugar. Definitely a kids' thing.

Seasonal discipline helps maintain the tenets of Estonian dining. Despite the preservation of some foods, Estonians try to cook to season whenever possible. Hearty meat stews are reserved for winter months, whilst lightly grilled fish, salads and fresh fruit abound in the summer months. Seasonal foods taste better and are, of course, packed with more vitamins and minerals when picked fresh and eaten immediately after harvesting. Ingredients must be balanced and often less is more. The right blend of a few simple ingredients creates delicious, sumptuous dishes.

I love sauerkraut with potatoes and smoked meat. The more you warm it up the better it tastes. You can have it for three days in a row and it gets better every day. The flavours come out. Now that is really traditional.

One of the most important elements of the simple Estonian diet is bread:

Estonians are famous for their bread, really dark sour dough. It is said that you have to knead your bread until your knuckles bleed! Only then is it considered proper bread. We have lots of different doughs from pale rye to really black rye, and barley and sourdough to many flatbreads.

The Estonian equivalent of *"bon appétit"* is *"head isu sõbrad"* (may your bread last). There are many superstitions surrounding bread, some logical, others strange:

We have a lot of superstitions around bread as it has a lot of significance. If you drop it you have to kiss it when you pick it up. Nothing is wasted: old bread is made into a mead called "kally", a really strong alcoholic drink.

There are various celebrations marked by special meals throughout the year. On 10th November Estonians celebrate St. Martin's Day, marking the end of the agrarian year and the beginning of winter. On that day most families eat goose, which is a symbol of St. Martin, a tradition that goes back to 1171. It is also common to eat grain such as barley, flour or blood sausage on St. Martin's Eve.

Today, Christmas is the most important festival of the year. Celebrations run from St. Thomas's Day (21st December) to Epiphany (6th January). Each year on 24th December, the President of Estonia declares Christmas Peace, a 350-year-old tradition, and then the real feasting begins. Traditional meals include *Sült* (jellied pork or veal), roast pork, salted or smoked meats, and blood puddings, beetroot salads, smoked or fresh herring, sprats, baked potatoes, mashed swede, wild mushrooms and sauerkraut, served with berry sauces and meat gravies, along with rye and ginger breads and honey beers. Traditionally, seven to twelve different meals are served on Christmas night. Eating enough food over Christmas symbolises the abundance of food you will have in the coming year. You certainly won't be hungry for a while if you follow this custom.

Blinchiki or Pannkoogid
Vodka Buckwheat Pancakes

Pirukad
Filled Pastries

Sült
Jellied Pork and Veal

Hernesupp
Pea and Gammon Soup with Sourdough Bread

Forell Hopulkoorega
Smoked Baltic Trout with Red Onion and Sour Cream

Rosolje
Beetroot Salad

Põrsa Praad Hapukapsaga
Roast Pork with Sauerkraut and Juniper Berries

Rukkileib
Dark Rye Bread

Verivorst
Black Pudding with Roast Potatoes and Lingonberry Jam

Kringel
Celebration Cake

Leivasupp Vanilla Kreemiga
Fruit Soup with Vanilla Cream

Magus Sai Või Kook
Gingerbread

Recipes

Blinchiki or Pannkoogid [Vodka Buckwheat Pancakes]

Blinchiki or Pannkoogid
Vodka Buckwheat Pancakes

This is a classic appetiser and well-known party food. Most people do not know what 'real' (read 'very expensive') caviar tastes like apart from being quite fishy. If you are one of them, like me, then standard fish roe is a great alternative. You can now find excellent brands in supermarkets and delicatessens and, of course, Ikea, my favourite source of Scandinavian-style foods. The pink or shiny black roe looks fabulous on the bright white soured cream and tastes delicious. The vodka makes the pancakes really crispy outside but smooth and fluffy inside.

125g butter	
2 large eggs, separated	Optional toppings:
700ml milk	Sour cream, caviar, fish roe, thin slivers of smoked salmon, flaked cooked trout, smoked herring, chopped gherkin, little sprigs of dill
250g buckwheat flour	
Pinch of salt	
Pinch of sugar	
2 tbsp vodka (optional)	
Oil for frying	

PREP:

1 Melt the butter

2 Spoon off 3 tablespoons of melted butter into a small cup or ramekin to be used later

3 Separate the eggs, saving the yolks and whites in separate bowls

4 Whisk the yolk and beat in the milk

5 Add the sifted buckwheat flour gradually, whisking all the time to make a smooth batter

6 Finally whisk in the melted butter, salt and sugar, then cover and leave the mix to thicken in the fridge for an hour

7 Whisk the egg whites until they form smooth peaks and can be held upside down without falling

8 Fold them into the rested batter with the vodka

COOK:

1. Heat the oil in a pan and spoon the batter into small rounds. You will need only 1 heaped tablespoon per *blinchiki*. Use the back of the spoon or lift and turn the pan to make the *blinchiki* round. When the bottom is brown and comes away from the pan easily, flip over and cook the other side

2. Have a plate ready for the cooked *blinchikis* and the cup of melted butter. As each *blinchiki* is cooked, remove from the pan, brush each side with butter and stack until ready to use

3. Serve with spoonfuls of sour cream topped with caviar, fish roe, thin slivers of smoked salmon or smoked herring and a little sprig of dill

Pirukad
Filled Pastries

These little pastries are enjoyed with beer and friends. They can be filled with pretty much anything but the favourite is lightly spiced meats with egg. Vegetarian versions are usually a combination of onion, mushrooms, carrots, swede, potato and cheese, or rice and egg. Instead of dicing the cooked meat and vegetables you can put them through a mincer creating a smoother, finer texture. Much like a Cornish pasty, these pastries were taken to work by farmers whose wives would have filled them with hearty but simple meat and vegetables, more often than not leftovers from the previous evening's meal.

Makes approx 20

1 packet of short crust pastry
or:
115g softened butter, 2 eggs, 5 tbsp buttermilk, 350g flour

3 Fillings:
(1) 250g cooked meat (ham, chicken, veal, or roast beef), 2 eggs, 1 onion, 1 tbsp butter, 1 tbsp paprika, salt and pepper

(2) 1 Onion, 1 carrot, ½ white cabbage, 2 tbsp butter, sprig of marjoram, salt and pepper

(3) Spinach, soft cheese such as quark or ricotta, ½ tsp nutmeg, salt and pepper

PREP:

1 In a large bowl mix one egg, buttermilk and butter, then sift in the flour mixing well. Refrigerate dough for an hour

2 Meanwhile prepare the meat pirukad filling: chop the meat into small cubes. Hard boil 2 eggs (about 8 minutes). Finely chop the onion then heat a tablespoon of butter in a pan, add the paprika and sauté the chopped onion. Dice the cooked egg. Remove pan from the heat and allow the mix to cool before combining the fried onion, meat and egg.

Season well with salt and pepper

3 For the vegetarian filling, peel and dice the onion, carrot and cabbage into small squares, fry in butter with a sprig of marjoram and season well with salt and pepper

4 Steam the spinach in a steamer or microwave for 2 minutes until the leaves have wilted, drain and squeeze out as much water as possible. Season with salt, pepper and freshly grated nutmeg, combine with quark and mix well

5 Grease a baking tray or line it with greased baking paper

COOK:

1. Sprinkle flour over counter or pastry board, roll dough evenly, and cut into long rectangles about 15cm wide

2. Along one edge, place teaspoons of fillings 5cm from the edge and 10cm apart

3. Brush a little egg onto the outer edges of the pastry and fold over the dough to cover the filling

4. Cut out semi-circles of the filled dough with a glass or pastry cutter

5. Pinch the open edges tightly together around the filling to squash out the air

6. Brush the top and edges of the pastries with some lightly beaten egg. Repeat filling and cutting until all the dough is used up

7. Place on the lined baking tray and bake at 180°C for 15 minutes or until lightly browned

Pirukads are incredible. They are delicious. I loved the carrot and cabbage ones but you can fill them with meat, spinach, mushrooms, egg, anything really. One popular traditional dish is to have pickled fish or sprats.

Sült
Jellied Pork and Veal

Sült is traditionally served at Christmas and in wintertime. It is usually made in large quantities because it keeps extremely well. It is referred to as brawn and in some American recipes as 'headcheese'. The traditional recipe uses pig's head and trotters but as these are difficult to find I have replaced them with standard cuts of meat and gelatine made with the stock from the meat. You should make a couple of litres of the stock as your terrine may be larger than mine and it is better to throw some away than have to start from scratch.

If you are fortunate enough to live or work near a farm shop or a good butcher it is definitely worth trying to find the original ingredients. If you succeed you won't need the gelatine as it will be produced by the natural marrows and gelatine in the meat. *Sült* can be dressed with white wine vinegar to taste, and served with pickled vegetables and warm potatoes with a large dollop of mustard.

Serves 5-6

250g gammon	Handful of black peppercorns
250g saddle of veal	2 tbsp allspice berries
1 onion	4 bay leaves
About 12 cloves	Gelatine leaves (usually 5 per litre of liquid)
Salt and freshly ground pepper	

PREP:

1 Chop all meat into big cubes and soak in cold water for 1 hour

2 Peel the onion and stud with the cloves

COOK:

1. Transfer the meat to a large cooking pot and cover with fresh cold water

2. Season with salt and pepper then add the peppercorns, allspice berries and studded onion

3. Bring to the boil, skimming the foam or scum that forms on top, then simmer uncovered on medium heat until the meat is done. This will take approximately 1 1/2 hours. The meat should break up in your fingers if you try to crumble it

4. Strain, saving the cooking liquid

5. De-bone the meat and cut it into smaller cubes

6. Prepare the gelatine according to the instructions on the packet. Use the slightly cooled cooking liquid to make about 2 litres

7. Put the meat cubes into a large terrine or jam jars and cover completely with jelly stock

8. Chill in the fridge until the texture is firm, then turn out and slice

Hernesupp [Pea and Gammon Soup with Sourdough Bread]

Hernesupp

Pea and Gammon Soup with Sourdough Bread

This is probably the best known Estonian traditional soup served in wintertime. A perfect restorative dish that is rich, creamy, and filled with vitamins and minerals to see you through the coldest days. As the peas and pork can be quite sweet it is delicious served with a sourdough bread or *leib*, Estonian black bread. Reheating makes it taste even better.

Serves 4

100g mild cure gammon	140g peas
1½ litres of water	50g butter
3 bay leaves	A handful of dill and flat leaf parsley
A large pinch of salt	A few glugs of olive oil
Twists of black pepper	Sourdough bread or *leib* (black bread)
1 carrot, roughly chopped	
1 onion, finely chopped	

PREP:

1 Roughly chop the carrot and finely chop the onion

2 Chop the dill and parsley

3 Toast the sourdough bread

COOK:

1. Place the gammon in a large pot, cover with the cold water, add the bay leaves, season with salt and pepper, and bring to the boil

2. Add half the carrot and onion to the stock and simmer for 2 hours, skimming foam or scum from the top during cooking

3. Strain the stock, reserving the gammon, which you then dice into smaller cubes. Cover and set aside

4. Reheat the stock and add peas to create a soup base

5. Meanwhile, in a pan, fry the remaining onion and carrot in butter until they caramelise well, then add to the soup base

6. Cook for 15 minutes so the peas soften, stir frequently to break the mixture down until the texture of the soup is creamy and even. Blend well and keep warm until ready to serve

7. Pre-heat the grill, brush the toasted sourdough with olive oil and grill until crisp and golden on both sides

8. Before serving the soup add warm gammon cubes and garnish with chopped herbs. Serve with the sourdough toast or black rye bread

I love this soup; it is really rich, which you don't expect, and tastes divine. Mum used to make it loads when we were growing up. I remember coming back home to the thick green soup bubbling away on the stove

Forell Hopulkoorega
Smoked Baltic Trout with Red Onion and Sour Cream

Baltic trout is one of the finest in Europe. It is eaten fresh, salted or smoked, and included in almost all traditional Estonian national dishes. This one highlights the quality of the fish by pairing it simply with sweet red onion and sour cream and serving it over potatoes, as it would be served in fishermen's homes across the nation. It is a fabulous summer dish.

1 red onion	A handful of Charlotte potatoes per person
1 tbsp capers	A drizzle of extra virgin olive oil
1 tbsp white wine vinegar	
1 bay leaf	Salt and pepper
Sprig of dill	200g smoked trout fillet
200ml sour cream	

PREP:

1 Finely chop the red onion and capers and soak with the vinegar and bay leaf for half an hour

2 Finely chop the dill

3 Remove the bay leaf and drain the onion. Mix it with the dill and sour cream

COOK:

1. Boil the potatoes until you can slide a knife through them, drain and allow to cool slightly

2. Slice and drizzle over a little olive oil, season with salt and pepper, mix well

3. Pile a few warm potatoes in the middle of the plate, place the fillets of smoked trout on top, spoon over a little onion, dill and sour cream; follow with a drizzle of olive oil round the plate and serve

Rosolje
Beetroot Salad

The *rosolje* salad is a jewel of Estonian cooking: beautiful, bright and simple. The beetroot juice colours the salad pink and the tangy lemon and pickles lift the flavour of the beetroot. You can make it with or without herring, according to your taste. Why not serve it accompanied by a glass of ice cold vodka infused with caraway seeds for a more European touch?

Makes 6 portions

4 beetroot	250ml sour cream
3 medium potatoes	1 tsp cider or white wine vinegar
2 apples	1 tsp Dijon mustard
½ lemon	Salt and pepper
2 dill pickles	
100g pickled herring (optional)	

PREP:

1 Boil the beetroot and potatoes in their skins until a knife slides through them easily (about 30 minutes), then peel, allow to cool and cube

2 Peel, core and cube the apple. Squeeze the lemon juice over

3 Dice the dill pickle

4 Finely slice the herring

COOK:

1. Mix all the diced ingredients in a large bowl

2. In a separate bowl make the dressing by whisking together the sour cream, mustard and vinegar, and season with salt and pepper

3. Pour over the salad and mix well so that it turns a beautiful shade of pink

Põrsa Praad Hapukapsaga
Roast Pork with Sauerkraut and Juniper Berries

Choosing the right cut of pork for slow roasting is essential. If you have to buy from a supermarket rather than a butcher pick up a few pieces and compare them. It's easy to see how different they can be. Also, beware of loins of rolled meat that have fat tied to them. The fat may not have come from the same animal. If possible get outdoor reared, organic pork. It is so different from the watery meat of shed reared animals.

Choose a cut with a deep layer of fat under the skin. This should look dry and the meat dark red and firm. People recommend 'rib end' or 'fillet end' but as long as it is a good loin this is secondary. There are two simple things necessary for fantastic crackling: a dry rind, and a thick layer of fat underneath it. You must score it deeply, use a stanley knife rather than the average kitchen knife to give you more grip and depth. This ensures that the fat will crisp up all the way through.

Serves 4

1.5kg pork loin	80g juniper berries
4 small apples	100ml vegetable stock
1 large onion	30g sugar
1 large white cabbage	1 tbsp caraway seeds
5-6 sage leaves	50ml vinegar

PREP:

1 Score the skin of the pork and season well with salt and pepper

2 Core the apples and score the skin so that they don't burst while roasting

3 Slice the onions into thick rings

4 Clean and shred the cabbage

COOK:

1. Pre-heat the roasting tin with oil, throw in the onions, bay leaf and juniper berries, and lie the loin on top

2. Roast in a very hot oven (250°C) for 20 minutes to start the fat bubbling under the skin and the crackling process

3. Add the apples, cover and reduce the heat to 180°C. Cook for 1 hour, basting occasionally with the appley juices

4. Heat some oil in a pan and fry the cabbage on a high heat until it has wilted a little and is beginning to caramelise, then add the sugar, caraway seeds and vinegar, toss well and add the stock. Reduce the heat to allow the cabbage to soften and braise for 15 minutes

5. Take the roasting tin out of the oven and remove the apples. Increase the temperature again and give the meat a final 20 minutes to really crisp up the fat. Cover the mean with foil and let it rest.

6. Meanwhile create the delicious gravy by draining the fat from the juices and deglazing the roasting tin, i.e. add a little wine or stock and pick up all the caramelised apple bits and onion with a wooden spoon

Rukkileib
Dark Rye Bread

Bread made solely from rye flour does not rise very well so it is mixed with wheat flour. If you want to keep it as dark as possible or have wheat intolerance try buckwheat flour. The taste of the rye will dominate but the bread will rise a little more, making it more versatile. Estonians don't mess with their black breads or *leib* – they are strong, really bitter, and can be quite over-powering to our palate.

2 tsp active dry yeast	3 tbsp unsweetened cocoa powder
1 tbsp brown sugar	1 tsp salt
2 tbsp molasses (optional)	100g butter or margarine
300ml water	1 tbsp caraway seed (optional)
140g rye flour	1 tsp fennel seed (optional)
350g strong bread flour or buckwheat flour	

PREP:

1 Prepare yeast according to packet directions. If it is fast action yeast, mix with the sugar and molasses and stir in enough water to dissolve the yeast to a thick cream

2 Sift the flours (keeping one tablespoon back for later), cocoa powder and salt into a large bowl and make a well in the centre

3 Tip the prepared yeast, a little water and the butter or margarine into the well

4 Stir the mixture well to make a soft dough

5 Turn out the dough onto a floured surface and knead for 10 to 15 minutes until you have smooth, non-sticky, elastic dough. Lastly work in the seeds

6 Put into a clean bowl and cover with cling film

7 Leave in a warm place to rise for a couple of hours until it has doubled in size

8 Turn it out again and knead for a couple more minutes

9 Shape into a loaf and put on a buttered, lined baking tray or loaf tin. Slash the top of the loaf into whatever pattern you fancy, then dust with the tablespoon of flour you reserved earlier

COOK:

1. Bake in a pre-heated 200°C oven for 30 minutes or until the crust is hard and the dough sounds hollow when tapped

Bread is so important in Estonian culture and cuisine that the pre-meal courtesy is "Jätku Leiba" or "May your bread last".

Verivorst

Black Pudding with Roast Potatoes and Lingonberry Jam

This is a traditional dish served for family feasts, weddings and *Jõulud* (Yuletide), the pagan feast celebrated over the Christmas period. Barley is one of the most common grains in Estonian cooking and this is a traditional way to use it. You have to be pretty brave to make black pudding but if you feel like pushing the boundaries of your comfort zone then this is something to try. Thankfully there are excellent Baltic and Scottish black puddings on the market so it you prefer not to see the raw ingredients you can cook only the accompaniments from scratch.

Black Pudding for the brave and the bold:	Roast Potatoes:
2 onions	50g goose fat or butter and oil mixed
400g smoked bacon	1 kg potatoes
500g pearl barley	Salt
2 litres water	Lingonberry Jam:
Salt	400g lingonberries or cranberries
100g lard or butter	200g sugar
1 litre fresh pig's blood	
500g thin casing	
Allspice	
Black pepper	
Marjoram	

PREP:

1 Chop the onions

2 Cube the bacon

3 Rinse the barley in cold water

4 Preheat the oven to 200°C

5 Peel the potatoes and chop them into large pieces

COOK:

[Part 1] Black Pudding

1. Put the barley and bacon in a large pot. Cover with water and season. Cook until it looks like porridge

2. In a separate pan, fry the onions in butter or lard, then combine with the bacon and barley and chill

3. Add the strained blood. Mix well and add black pepper and marjoram. Fill the casing tightly, tie into a sausage shape, securing the ends with string

4. Bring the sausage to the boil in water seasoned with allspice. After 20 minutes poke one end with a cocktail stick. It is done when the juices run clear. Drain and place in a small roasting tin. Set aside

[Part 2] Finished Dish

1. Parboil the potatoes in salted water for 10 minutes, drain crushing the edges a little (this makes them crunchier)

2. Preheat a roasting tin in the oven with the goose fat and roast the potatoes at 180°C for 45 minutes

3. Meanwhile, prepare the jam by bringing the berries and sugar to the boil, stirring so that the jam does not catch on the bottom. Take off the heat when it has the consistency of loose porridge. Allow to cool. It will become thicker as it sets

4. Finish cooking the black pudding by roasting it in the preheated oven for 15 minutes until the skin is crisp

5. Slice and serve with roast potatoes and plenty of jam

Kringel
Celebration Cake

This is a beautiful, golden sweet bread often given as a gift to celebrate a special occasion such as a birth or wedding. The dough is formed into a plait or pretzel shape and brushed with golden egg, then topped with lightly toasted almonds. Saffron is also used in the mix to symbolise the sun and a new dawn.

1½ sachets dried yeast	1 pinch of saffron
125ml water	900g plain flour
1 tsp green cardamom pods	225g butter
500ml milk	1 egg, beaten
500g sugar	2 tbsp flaked almonds
1 tsp salt	1 tbsp icing sugar
5 egg yolks	

PREP:

1 Dissolve the yeast in a little warm water

2 In a pestle and mortar crush the cardamom pods. Throw away the husks leaving the seeds

3 Warm the milk and stir in the sugar, salt, cardamom seeds and egg yolks and a pinch of saffron

4 Sift the flour into another bowl, make a well in it and pour in the liquid ingredients, combining them well to make a smooth dough

5 Add the melted butter and beat again until a stiff dough
6 forms

7 Turn out onto a floured board and knead well, then cover with a bowl and allow to rest for 15 minutes

8 Knead the dough again lightly until it is smooth and shiny, then return it to a greased mixing bowl, cover lightly, and let it prove again until it has doubled in size. This will take about 1 hour. Do this twice

9 Turn out on a floured board and form into two plaited loaves or pretzel shapes

10 Glaze the *kringel* with the beaten egg
Sprinkle over the flaked almonds

COOK:

1. Bake in a pre-heated oven at about 190°C for 1 hour

2. Dust with icing sugar and serve

Leivasupp Vanilla Kreemiga
Fruit Soup with Vanilla Cream

Many Baltic states serve hot and cold fruit soups for breakfast, snacks or as a separate course in a meal. In Sweden it is served before fish; in Norway it is served after game but in Estonia fruit soup is most often served as a dessert. This is almost a liquid fruit cake, rich with plum brandy and dark berries.

Fruit soups were apparently extremely fashionable on the tables of knights, aristocrats and even royalty throughout Europe at the time of the crusades, the idea having been borrowed from Persia. The fashion faded, as fashions do, and the dish lost its place at the elegant table and became a staple for peasants and farmers who used any dried fruits they had mixed with limited fresh fruit to create its distinctive flavour.

The Baltic States have retained their taste for the sweet and sour combination in food and still feature many fruits in main dishes.

70g raisins	1.5 litres water
70ml plum or apple brandy (or brandy)	80g sugar
6 thin slices black rye bread or sourdough	100g pitted dried prunes (or other dried fruit)
2 sharp apples	60g cranberries
1 lemon	150ml cranberry juice
1 vanilla pod	1 cinnamon stick
120-200ml double cream	4 cloves

PREP:

1 Soak the raisins by pouring hot water over them, then drain and put in a bowl with the brandy until they are plump. This will take about 40 minutes

2 Cut the crusts off the bread and toast it until it is crisp

3 Peel and core the apples, then cut into small chunks

4 Grate the zest of the lemon

5 Deseed the vanilla pod

6 Whip the double cream and stir through the vanilla seeds

COOK:

1. In a large saucepan bring the water to the boil, stir in the sugar and bring to a rolling boil for 1 minute

2. Add the bread, reduce the heat and simmer until the bread begins to break up

3. Scoop out the bread with a slotted spoon and sieve it back into the pot

4. Stir in the soaked raisins with all the brandy juices, the apples, prunes, cranberries, cranberry juice, cinnamon stick and cloves, and the lemon zest

5. Bring to the boil, then reduce heat, cover, and simmer for 15 minutes on a low heat until the fruit is tender

6. For a smooth texture put it through a blender, or simply allow it to cool, then refrigerate until ready to serve topped with a spoonful of the vanilla cream

Everyone has a summer house in Estonia. They are rows of houses like you would have in England not country cottages in the middle of nowhere. Everyone goes there for a couple of months if they can. My nana used to grow everything there: apple trees, cherry trees, strawberries, all the fruit and vegetables you could think of. She dried or preserved all the fruit that was not eaten.

Magus Sai Või Kook
Gingerbread

Gingerbread is the perfect accompaniment for a glass of mulled wine, headily spiced to make your cheeks rosy and warm you from the inside out. Both are enjoyed throughout the winter and are made in abundance to be offered to guests.

300g flour	Pinch of salt
2 tsp baking powder	1 tsp ground cinnamon
1 egg	1 tsp ground ginger
100g sugar	½ tsp ground cloves
250g honey (or treacle)	½ tsp cardamom
50g butter	½ tsp nutmeg

<u>PREP:</u>

1 Sieve the flour with the baking powder so it is evenly distributed

2 Whisk the egg

3 Butter a baking sheet

4 Preheat the oven to 200°C

COOK:

1. In a heavy-bottomed saucepan melt the honey or treacle

2. When it is boiling, add the sugar, butter and salt. Bring to the boil again, stirring all the time

3. Add the spices, then turn off the heat and allow the mixture to cool before adding the egg

4. Once well cooled whisk in the egg and gradually add the flour, at first mixing with a spoon but eventually kneading with your hands to create a firm dough

5. Allow the dough to rest for about 10 minutes

6. On a floured surface roll the dough out and cut into whatever shape you like

7. Bake for 12-15 minutes, until brown and slightly soft to the touch

8. Decorate when completely cool

The smell of the spices and honey really fills the house. We made them as children and would prepare a batch to go on the Christmas tree. We poked a hole in the biscuits with a pencil so we could thread red ribbon through but once on the tree they rarely made it to Christmas Day — they were just too good to resist.

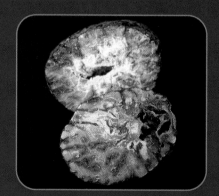

An Ethiopian
Kitchen

Introduction to an Ethiopian Kitchen

A complex of mountains, plateaux and semi-desert divided by the Great Rift Valley make up the terrain that is Ethiopia. Although there are climatic changes from area to area, the burning sun is a constant, so much so that Ethiopia was once known as 'the land of thirteen months of sunshine'.

Ethiopia's civilisation is one of the oldest in the world. Sustaining it for thousands of years was, of course, its food. Sadly, as most people know, over the last fifty years much of the country has been ravaged by war and famine. Despite this Ethiopians, especially those living outside their homeland, are encouraging others to look beyond their immediate troubled history to discover a noble and precious cuisine, in the hope that it will give a new generation an insight into one of the splendours of their culture.

Ethiopia is somewhat removed geographically from the rest of the continent, lying on what is known as the Great Horn of Africa. The mountains surrounding it both protect and isolate it from its neighbours. Its cuisine can therefore be considered one of Africa's purest.

Despite its isolation it held a strategic position on the ancient trade routes, particularly those linked to Arab nations such as Yemen. The trade routes brought spices and herbs to Ethiopia including chilli, cardamom, cinnamon, turmeric and cloves. These were readily incorporated into its cuisine and give most Ethiopian dishes their characteristic heat, an intense, rich heat that moves from palate to nose then deep into the sinuses, leaving any unaccustomed diner rather rosycheeked.

In return for these spices, Ethiopians gave the world the great gift of coffee. Originating in the Kaffa highlands of south-west Ethiopia, the native Arabica tree has been

harvested by tribespeople and goat herders for centuries. Legend has it that a goat herder noticed that when his goats nibbled the coffee berries they had an extra spring in their step that seemed to last all night. Curious, he ate a few of the berries himself, crunching through the pale green beans inside. Not long afterwards he felt his heart beating faster and was overcome by an immense feeling of lucidity. The berries have been popular ever since and their potent properties used and abused by men and women all over the world.

Ethiopian blends of coffee are now world renowned but roasting and brewing the beans did not become popular in Europe until the fourteenth century. In an age when organic products are in favour, it is comforting to know more that ninety per cent of the coffee harvested in Ethiopia is apparently still organically grown. Flavours range from the fruity *ghimbi*, the winy *limu*, the almost cheesy *illubabor*, the mocha *yirga cheffe*, to the fine blueberry undertones of the *harar*.

The temperate climate, high interior plains, and long seasons are also ideally suited to the cultivation of another potent grain, *teff*, the smallest grain in the world and arguably the most important one in the Ethiopian diet. Its name literally translates as 'lost'. Almost completely gluten free, high in amino acids, fibre, iron, calcium, potassium and a number of other minerals it is classed as a 'superfood'. Ethiopians grind it to a flour and make it into light, pancake-like *injera*, which they use as a plate, cutlery substitute, and as a filling accompani-ment to every meal.

The Coptic Church, the dominant religious sect in Ethiopia since the fourth century, dictates many Ethiopian food customs. Fasts play a more important part than feasting in Ethiopian dining culture, with over two hundred fasting days a year. This frequent banning of meat has led to the evolution of a dynamic and varied vegetarian cuisine. From bean stews, 'false banana', chick pea fritters, pickled cabbages, flavoured curds to fragrant greens, cooks have created a plethora of foods to stave off hunger and please the palate without upsetting the gods.

Flavours of an Ethiopian Kitchen

Ethiopian cuisine is characterised by the lavish use of strong spices. An essential element in creating this unique flavour is a paste called *berbere*: a thick red blend of up to twenty ingredients that almost always include paprika, salt, ginger, onion, garlic, cloves, cinnamon, nutmeg, cardamom, allspice, pepper, coriander, and fenugreek, all expertly ground down with water and a little oil. Today most Ethiopian cooks buy their *berbere* from the supermarket or a deli but homemade blends are fresher and more pungent.

Alongside *berbere*, *nitter kibbeh* or spiced butter is used in creating authentic Ethiopian flavour is . Unlike the creamy fresh butter pats in Europe, *kibbeh* is usually sold in bitter slabs that are clarified and combined with spices, onions, garlic and ginger according to taste at home. *Berbere*, *kibbeh* and other blends such as the spicy *awaze* and *mitmitta* are integral to most Ethiopian recipes, yet different dishes have carefully attuned degrees of heat. A good way to remember is that a *wot* is hot; for those who prefer a milder stew *alicha* is not.

Pork is not a favoured meat because of common Coptic Orthodox beliefs but goat, lamb, beef and chicken are found in abundance. The freshness of the meat is extremely important to all cooks and meat will often be slaughtered to order. At traditional Ethiopian weddings, the bride and groom often serve fresh slices of raw beef to their guests. A more popular everyday dish is *kitfo*, raw spiced ground beef served with assorted condiments.

Cooked food was traditionally prepared in large black or brown clay pots and these are still favoured for some dishes in modern kitchens. When making *shiro*, for example, the clay pot is said to add a smoky flavour that gives the dish more depth and warmth.

The diet is lightened by an abundance of fruit (bananas, grapes, pomegranates, dates, figs, custard apples) and vegetables of all kinds, including the wonderful red onions, used by the bag in such dishes as *doro wot*, and a strong kale-like plant used in the *alicha*. Other vegetarian dishes are based on pulses, grains and legumes, especially lentils and chick peas. These are cooked and eaten as salads, seasoned and added to *wots*, or dried and ground into flour to be used, inter alia, as a base for vegetarian fritters.

Ethiopians were not only the first to produce and popularise coffee, they were also among the first to domesticate bees and use honey in everyday food and medicine. The most famous Ethiopian drink apart from coffee is *tej* – a fragrant, sweet honey wine brewed in the same way as old English mead. Ethiopia is known as the 'land of milk and honey'. Queens bathed in it, physicians prescribed it, and cooks … well cook it!

Contents of an Ethiopian Store Cupboard

Cloves

Cumin

Garlic

Ginger

Cardamom

Cinnamon

Black Peppercorns

Allspice

Fenugreek

Paprika

Chilli

Mint

Parsley

Coriander

Vanilla

Honey

Nitter kibbeh (Spiced Butter)

Berbere Paste

Awaze Paste

Mitmitta Paste

Onions

Teff

Buckwheat Flour

Lentils

Wheat

Yeast

Sorghum Flour

Cabbage

Spinach

Cottage Cheese

Tomatoes

Eggs

Green Beans

Kale

Collard Greens

Limes

Lemons

Pomegranates

Lessons learnt along the way…

Eating Ethiopian style is a very intimate and welcoming experience made up of a blend of religious ritual and honest hospitality. The diet is varied and rich in flavours with a variety of meat, eggs and pulses served in small portions on *injera*.

Breakfast is something dry, like a fit fit, with the injera inside it. We also cook a dish that has meat inside the egg, a sort of omelette with onions and tomato. We pour over a hot thick, red sauce made with lots of berbere. We might also have dullet; finely chopped lambs' tripe with lambs' liver and a little red beef. The rest of the dishes, usually the wetter ones can be served for lunch or dinner any time.

To balance their diet, Ethiopians are not concerned about having one meat to one vegetable dish. Dinner will often consist of three meat dishes to one vegetarian dish.

What we might do is if we have meat at lunch we won't eat it again for dinner. We might have something lighter like a shiro or some spinach. We eat fresh salad regularly: big plates of lettuce and tomato as well as vegetarian dishes. We eat boiled potato and carrots served cold with lemon but we don't call it a salad. Traditionally all vegetarian dishes are served cold. Here, we serve them warm, perhaps because of the climate but back home anything with vegetables in it would be cold. They say it tastes better.

In many traditional households, family and guests sit on cushions or a divan round a *mesab* (a low table). This is made of wicker and is shaped like an hourglass. Hands must be washed before and after the meal, the religious significance no doubt born out of the same practicality and hygiene that dictates Ethiopians must eat with their right hand. These days the rules are not so stringent.

It is pretty relaxed. If you are left handed you eat with your left hand and the other one rests on the table or on your lap. Like anywhere you are not supposed to put your elbows on the table but it would be hard to do this anyway if you were eating from the mesab as it is only big enough for the tray of food.

Injera is brought in on a large platter or tray and placed on the table in front of the guests. Individual platters and bowls of curries and vegetables are brought by the hostess who will serve a spoonful to each person in turn on the *injera* so that they have their portions directly in front of them. Often an extra basket of *injera* is brought for people to get started. You tear off a little *injera*, use it to pick up small morsels of food and mop up some sauce then pop it into your mouth. With practice, your fingers don't even touch your lips, ensuring a cleaner more attractive dining experience. Ethiopians eat modestly and as they dine from the same 'plate' as other people it is easy to see who is being greedy

You should take care not to reach over someone when you are eating. The hostess will usually put spoonfuls of things in front of you so you have your own section of the injera. Reaching over would be like eating from someone else's plate. It depends who you are eating with; in polite company you would never do it but if it is family you might get away with it.

An old Ethiopian proverb says, "*People who eat from the same plate will never betray one another.*" When you eat from the *injera*, you are conscious not only of the food in front of you but of the others who are sharing your 'plate'. Also there is no waste: everything is eaten.

The final part of the meal is often a raw meat dish called a *kifto*, served with yogurt and a traditional curd cheese. When all the stews and foods have been eaten and the last of the soft, juice soaked *injera* enjoyed, dinner is over. No dessert is served at this stage, just coffee and cereals. Later, if you are still hungry, you might have some sweet pastries, similar to *baklava*, small treats dipped in honey and covered in nuts.

Coffee plays a significant part in the Ethiopian diet and social mores. The coffee ceremony is as advanced as the Japanese tea ceremony but less formal. It is still played out in homes and restaurants three times a day: at breakfast, at lunch and before dinner. The ceremony begins as the hostess washes the green coffee beans. She will then place them in a pan and roast them over a flame. Once roasted a little water is sprinkled over them releasing the heady aroma, which is enjoyed by all the guests as the pan is passed round. The beans are then ground in a pestle and mortar called a *mukecha*, before being brewed in a *jabena*, an earthenware pot preferred to modern metallic pots. Coffee can be brewed to three different strengths from the lightest *bereka buna* to the medium *helegna buna*, to the strongest *abola buna*. The usually thick brew will then be poured into small handle-less cups called *sinne*. There should be enough coffee for three cups per guest.

Coffee is always served with roasted cereals such as barley and nuts. Outside Ethiopia you are more likely to be served popcorn with your coffee. The end of your meal should be as fragrant as the moment when the food is served so the host will burn incense while everyone washes their hands once again.

As this rather intricate way of serving even a simple supper suggests, Ethiopians are a very social people who often have to cater for large extended families:

For celebrations there is always a massive spread. Cooks really go to town. You would always have a

doro wot, another chicken dish, lamb and beef dishes as well as about twenty vegetarian dishes. Celebrations are presented buffet style so people take some injera and help themselves. Usually the grown-ups eat together and the children eat together.

A small wedding would cater for no less than fifty to a hundred people and for a large wedding or funeral the hosts might be expected to provide food for over a thousand guests. It is not surprising then that the dishes are easy-to-prepare one-pot wonders best served to large groups of people. They are prepared in advance and allowed to simmer away slowly on the fire. This makes Ethiopian food my ultimate tried and tested party food; all that needs to be done is for the hostess to take bowls of the stews to the *injera*, serve it and sit back and enjoy it as the feast begins; even the plates are eaten.

Recipes

Berbere and Nitter Kibbeh
Ethiopian Red Spice Blend and Spiced Butter

Injera
Sourdough Bread, Cutlery, Plate!

Doro Wot
Chicken and Boiled Egg in a Fiery Ethiopian Sauce

Shiro
Spicy Split Pea Stew

Ya Beg Alicha Fit Fit
Mild and Fragrant Lamb Stew

Misser Wot
Spiced Lentil Stew

Abish
Beef with Tomato and Herbs

Yetesom Beyaynetu
Spiced vegetables

Awaze Tibs
Lean Cubed Lamb with Onion, Bullet Chilli and Berbere

Ayib Be Gomen
Spinach with Spiced Cottage Cheese

Kitfo
Steak Tartare

Berbere and Nitter Kibbeh
Ethiopian Red Spice Blend and Spiced Butter

There are, of course, many different blends of spices that make up the *berbere*. The characteristic red colour comes from the paprika so this acts as the most substantial base; then numerous other traditional flavours of Ethiopian cooking are incorporated. If you are one or two ingredients short, don't worry; just keep on tasting the blend and you'll know what you want to add next time. You can use the *berbere* immediately or store it in a jar. Ethiopians often gently pour a thin layer of pure oil over the paste to act as a sealant when storing it. This oil is poured off and replenished each time the berbere is used to ensure its purity.

The heat of the *berbere* is so intense you must be careful not to rub your eyes while making it or you will cry for a week. If your hands are dyed or still fragrant from the spices even after you have washed them a few times try rubbing lemon all over them, then rinsing. It works for me.

Berbere (Red Spice Blend)	
1 tsp ground ginger	1 small onion
1/2 tsp cardamom	2 cloves of garlic
1/2 tsp coriander	2 tsp salt
1/2 tsp fenugreek	1 1/2 cups of water
1/2 tsp nutmeg	100g paprika
1/2 tsp cloves	1/2 tsp red pepper
1/2 tsp cinnamon	2 tbsp black pepper
1/2 tsp crushed allspice	2 tbsp vegetable oil

PREP:

1 Mince onion and garlic

COOK:

1. In a dry pan toast ginger, cardamom, coriander, fenugreek, nutmeg, cloves, cinnamon and allspice for 1-2 minutes, stirring constantly

2. Remove from the heat and let spices cool

3. Combine toasted spices, onion, garlic, 1 tsp of salt and a little water. Blend in a pestle and mortar (if you have one, if not a food processor or blender is fine), until a smooth paste is formed

4. In the same pan toast paprika, red pepper, black pepper and the other tsp of salt for 1 minute. Add water and stir to create a smooth liquid

5. Add the spice paste and stir vigorously. Cook over a really low heat for about 10 minutes

6. Store in a jar that has been heated in the oven or boiled to kill any bacteria

If you have berbere and kibbeh you can make anything Ethiopian

COOK:

1. In a large saucepan, melt the butter slowly over medium heat to prevent colouration

2. Bring it to the boil and when it is foaming add onion, garlic, ginger, turmeric, cardamom, cinnamon, cloves, and nutmeg

3. Reduce the heat and simmer uncovered and undisturbed for 45 minutes. The milk solids will sink to the bottom of the pan and turn golden brown while the butter on top will be clarified and transparent

4. Strain through a cheesecloth (or if you don't have one, pour slowly through your finest sieve stopping before any milk solids pass through the holes)

5. Transfer to a clean, dry jar, cover tightly and store in the refrigerator ready for use

Nitter Kibbeh (Spiced Butter)	
1 onion	1 tsp ground cardamom
4 cloves garlic	1 tbsp ground cinnamon
3 tbsp ground ginger	3 cloves
900g butter	1/2 tsp freshly grated nutmeg
1 tbsp turmeric	

PREP:

1 Peel and mince onion and garlic in a blender, or grate

Injera [Sourdough Bread, Cutlery, Plate!]

Injera

Sourdough Bread, Cutlery, Plate!

It is easy to see how one grain can be the staple food of a nation. *Teff* is an excellent source of essential amino acids, fibre and iron, and contains many times the amount of calcium, potassium and other essential minerals found in an equal amount of other grains. *Teff* is also low in gluten so it is very easily digested. Perfect if you are watching your weight or have issues with other bread products.

Teff is available in some health food stores and specialist grocers but a great *injera* can still be made from normal flour. If you made this bread every day you would treat is as a sourdough, keeping a little mixture back each time and allowing it to ferment to mix into the next day's batter. I don't imagine you will, just as most Ethiopians don't nowadays. Instead use some sparkling water, which has the same effect.

You can give each person their own *injera* but this goes against the communal feel of Ethiopian dining so cover a large tray or even your coffee table with cling film and arrange the *injera* so that they overlap and cover the whole surface. Bring the curries and dishes to the table in bowls and spoon a serving on the *injera* in front of each guest. You may want to keep a couple back and cut them into strips to give your guests something to start with so by the time they use the 'tablecloth' there is less food on it.

Makes 8

280g flour	500ml sparkling water
½ tsp baking powder	

PREP:

1 Mix flour and baking powder in a large bowl

2 Add the sparkling water gradually, pulling in the flour to ensure a smooth thin batter

COOK:

1. Heat a large non-stick pan and brush lightly with oil

2. Using a cup or ladle, pour the batter into the pan. For a perfect round shape every time begin on the outside of the pan and work your way in, lift and turn the pan to fill in any holes and spread evenly

3. Cook for 1-2 minutes, until the surface is spongy and filled with tiny air bubbles

4. Do not flip the bread – just slide it off onto a large plate. Continue cooking *injera* until the batter is used up, transferring them to the plate as they are done

Doro Wot [Chicken and Boiled Egg in a Fiery Ethiopian Sauce]

Doro Wot
Chicken and Boiled Egg in a Fiery Ethiopian Sauce

Wot essentially means stew. As with most Ethiopian stews, *Doro Wot*, one of the best known, is made with *berbere* and *kibbeh*, a unique blend of toasted and simmered spices in butter. If you can't make up the *kibbeh* beforehand and can't buy it you can add a few teaspoons of cayenne pepper and paprika to the melted butter. It may not be as delicate or fragrant but at least gives the characteristic dark red colour and Ethiopian flavour.

Good quality chicken is important. Try to buy free range and, if possible, organically fed chickens; their meat contains less water and fat than battery chickens and so not only tastes better but is better for you.

Tear off a piece of *injera* flatbread and use it to scoop up the stew and pinch pieces of fresh plump chicken from the bone. You can also serve it with some lightly spiced cottage cheese and spinach on the side.

1.4kg chicken	3 tbsp vegetable oil
2cm ginger	2 tbsp *kibbeh* (or butter)
4 large onions	2 tbsp *berbere* paste
4 cloves of garlic	250ml chicken stock
4 eggs	2 tbsp lime juice

PREP:

1 Joint the chicken into 8 pieces. Rinse and pat dry with paper

2 Peel and chop the ginger, slice the onions and mince garlic

3 Hard boil the eggs (8-10 minutes), drop into iced water to stop the yolks turning black, then peel and set aside

COOK:

1. Heat the oil in a pan and brown the chicken. Once browned remove it with a slotted spoon

2. In the same pan add the *kibbeh* (or butter), onion, ginger and garlic, and gently fry until caramelised and glossy

3. Add *berbere* paste and cook for a further minute

4. Add stock and lime juice and simmer 3-4 minutes

5. Return the chicken to the pan, cover, and simmer slowly for 1 hour and 30 minutes, turning it from time to time. If the sauce looks too thick add more chicken stock, if too liquid for your taste remove the lid to allow the juices to reduce to a thick sauce

6. When it is cooked add the peeled hard boiled eggs and transfer the stew to a large bowl. Serve with *injera*, making sure each guest has an egg

At anyone's house for any type of festival you will always get Doro Wot. Back home we cook a whole chicken and break it up into small pieces, and if you have ten people then you would have ten eggs in it so everyone gets an egg and some chicken. It is so delicious it always reminds me of celebrations. We use lots of onions and roast the wot down for about 6 or 7 hours with lots of kibbeh and berbere.

Shiro
Spicy Split Pea Stew

Shiro is made traditionally with the ground yellow split peas that share their name with this dish. The spicy, sweet stew is very popular during the Lenten season as it is high in protein, full of flavour and quite filling. The consistency of shiro differs according to taste. When it is made from powder it has a smooth, creamy consistency but when it is made with whole split peas you get rich, dense dollops, aggressively seasoned. I prefer the thicker version as I think it tastes more natural. Blend a few tablespoons in an electric blender once it has cooked to see which texture and consistency you prefer.

2 onions	2 tsp paprika
2 cloves of garlic	1 tsp cayenne pepper
5cm ginger	450g yellow split peas (or chick peas)
1 tbsp *nitter kibbeh* (spiced butter)	500ml vegetable stock
1 tsp turmeric	Salt and pepper to taste
1 tbsp fenugreek	

PREP:

1 Finely chop onion, garlic, and ginger, or blend to a paste in an electric blender

COOK:

1. Heat the *nitter kibbeh* in a large saucepan

2. Add turmeric, fenugreek, paprika and cayenne pepper, and stir rapidly over a low heat to roast the spices

3. Add the onion, garlic and ginger paste, and fry on a medium heat until softened

4. Add the split peas and stock

5. Bring to a boil and simmer for 30-40 minutes, or until the peas are cooked through, adding water if necessary to keep them from drying out

6. Season with salt and pepper to taste and serve

Ya Beg Alicha Fit Fit

Mild and Fragrant Lamb Stew

Alicha is typically a milder alternative to the hot *wot*. Although this stew is flavoured with *berbere* the addition of cumin and cardamom lifts it from its rich base, and the vegetables and stock serve to make it wholesome and healthy. Ethiopians tear up their *injera* and add it to this dish soaking up the juices and creating a thicker stew.

2 carrots	Large pinch cumin seeds
1 red onion	Large pinch cardamom pods
2 cloves of garlic	1 medium lamb shank
1/2 white cabbage	600ml lamb stock
Oil	1/2 tsp turmeric
1 tbsp *berbere*	1 large *injera*

<u>PREP:</u>

1 Peel and dice the carrots and onion

2 Mince the garlic

3 Chop the cabbage into small cubes

COOK:

1. In a stove top casserole dish heat the oil and add the *berbere*

2. Add garlic, onion, cabbage and carrot with the cumin and cardamom and sauté to soften a little

3. Sear the lamb all over, then pour in the stock and stir in the turmeric, bring to the boil, then reduce the heat, cover and simmer for 1 hour and 30 minutes on low heat or until the lamb is tender

4. Tear up the *injera* and add it to the stew, stirring until it soaks up most of the juices. Cook for 10 minutes before serving

Misser Wot
Spiced Lentil Stew

Lentils simmered in a rich sauce deliver the smoky tang of a good barbecue with a beautiful hint of ginger. Pulses make up a large part of the Ethiopian diet during fast days. *Misser wot* is a particularly nutritious and tasty dish that is so filling that even the hardiest meat eater could not think of it as 'rabbit food'.

2 red onions	Salt and pepper
5 cm ginger	Generous tbsp ghee or a glug of oil
2 cloves of garlic	1 tbsp *berbere*
500g lentils	
Water	

PREP:

1 Peel and chop the onion, ginger, and garlic

COOK:

1. Put the lentils in a pot, cover with water and salt well. Bring the water to the boil and cook for 5 minutes

2. Drain, reserving the water

3. In a pan heat the ghee or oil, fry the *berbere*, garlic, and ginger until fragrant

4. Fry the onions until soft and add the drained lentils. Season, toss and fry for 1 minute

5. Add enough of the drained water to cover the lentils and an additional 1cm of water on top

6. Cover and simmer for 35 minutes stirring occasionally, tasting and adjusting seasoning if necessary

7. Serve with *injera*

Abish
Beef with Tomato and Herbs

This is one of the fresher Ethiopian style dishes, perfect for a light lunch. It goes well on some plain rice or served with an Ethiopian style salad of onion, tomato, and a few chopped chillies – jalapeno work well – all dressed with a little sunflower oil and lemon juice.

2 onions	Generous glug of oil
2 cm ginger	500g minced beef
1 clove of garlic	1 tsp turmeric
3 large tomatoes	Salt and pepper
A handful of mint	3 eggs
Large handful of parsley	200g soft goat's cheese (or ricotta)
150g butter	

PREP:

1 Peel and grate ginger

2 Peel and chop garlic and onions

3 Deseed and dice tomatoes

4 Finely chop mint and parsley and combine with butter, keeping a few leaves for garnish

COOK:

1. Heat the oil and fry the onions until they are soft and golden

2. Add the ginger, garlic and minced beef, and brown for a couple of minutes

3. Add the chopped tomatoes, season with turmeric, salt and pepper and cook for 10-15 minutes

4. Add eggs and cook for a further 10 minutes

5. Remove from the heat, season, then stir in the herby butter and goat's cheese and serve

Yetesom Beyaynetu
Spiced Vegetables

Perhaps because Coptic Ethiopians traditionally eat vegetarian food twice a week, the cuisine has developed a large variety of complex vegetarian dishes. *Yetesom beyaynetu* means 'vegetable combination' so you can use any combination of vegetables for this dish: cauliflower, cabbage and sweet potatoes are good alternatives as they hold their shape and texture in cooking. This recipe calls for a small amount of red chilli but you can omit it or increase the amount according to your taste.

6 small potatoes	1-2 small red chillies
3 carrots	6 spring onions
200g green beans	Salt and pepper to taste
2 cloves of garlic	Small bunch of coriander
2cm fresh ginger	80ml peanut or vegetable oil
2 onions	
1 green pepper	

PREP:

1 Peel potatoes and carrots and slice into 1cm strips, then cut into batons

2 Top and tail the green beans

3 Peel and mince the garlic and ginger

4 Peel and chop the onions

5 Deseed the green pepper and chop into batons

6 Deseed the chillies for a milder taste, then finely chop

7 Chop the spring onions into strips and roughly chop the coriander

COOK:

1. Bring a large pot of water to the boil. Add potatoes and carrots and bring back to the boil, then simmer for 15 minutes. Throw in the green beans five minutes before the end

2. Drain vegetables immediately and set aside

3. Heat the oil in a large pan and sauté the onions, green pepper and chilli until the onions begin to soften; then add garlic, ginger, spring onion, salt and pepper

4. Add the cooked vegetables and toss well to ensure they are completely coated in the seasonings. Cook for 5 minutes until the vegetables are piping hot

5. Serve topped with freshly chopped coriander

Awaze Tibs
Lean Cubed Lamb with Onion, Bullet Chilli and Berbere

I really love lamb and rosemary and was thrilled that Ethiopians also use this combination of kings, albeit with a 'bullet' chilli, *berbere* and plenty of pepper. Tender pieces of lamb are fried in the *berbere* spices cooked with mounds of golden onions.

500g lamb loin or neck fillets	1 bullet chilli (or strong green chilli)
5 onions	1 tbsp black peppercorns
2 green peppers	80ml oil
2 large sprigs of rosemary	1 tbsp *berbere*

PREP:

1 Cube the lamb into large chunks

2 Chop the onions

3 Deseed the peppers and chop roughly

4 Roughly chop the chilli and pull the rosemary leaves off the stalks and chop roughly

5 Pound both in a pestle and mortar with the black pepper

6 Add a little oil to the herb mix and marinate the meat in it for at least an hour

COOK:

1. Heat the oil in a large pan, add the meat with all the seasonings. Brown and stir in the *berbere*

2. Add peppers and onions to cover the lamb and allow them to cook through for 10 minutes, shaking the pan every now and then. Serve the lamb tender and slightly pink

TIP:
If you want to know if your lamb (or any meat) is done you can do the finger test:

Relax your hands. Place the index finger on the thumb of your left hand. Then with the index finger of your right hand push on the fleshy base of the left thumb – it will give a little; that is what rare meat should feel like. Now place the middle finger on the thumb of your left hand. Feel again and you will notice that it is slightly firmer – that is medium rare. Place your fourth finger on your thumb and you have medium. Place your little finger on your thumb and you have well done – overdone in my book.

Ayib Be Gomen

Spinach with Spiced Cottage Cheese

This is a great accompaniment to *kitfo* (raw spiced beef) or a stand-alone dish. Interestingly the combination of spinach and cheese is pretty global, with good reason: they complement each other perfectly. *Ayib* is a fairly grainy tasting cheese somewhere between a Greek feta and an English cottage cheese. Either can be used. The former is stronger and drier on the palate, the latter less dense. It is a matter of taste. In this dish the important thing is to strain and crumble the cheese before you use it. You'll need to strain the spinach well too. An easy way of doing this is to wrap it in a clean tea towel and wring it out. After wringing it a few times I often step outside and use some centrifugal force to help get the last of the water out by spinning it round and round – make sure you have a firm grip on it and watch out for your neighbours.

1 pack feta or a tub of cottage cheese	100g spinach or greens
4 tbsp natural yogurt	*Nitter kibbeh* or oil
2 tbsp parsley	Garlic
½ tsp ground cardamom	Ginger
Salt and pepper	1 chilli

PREP:

1 Mix cheese with yogurt, parsley, cardamom, salt and pepper

2 Wash spinach or greens thoroughly

COOK:

1. Steam spinach or greens until wilted, then squeeze out as much water as possible

2. In a separate pan heat some *nitter kibbeh* or oil; fry the garlic, ginger and chilli and toss in the spinach

3. Combine with the cheese mix and warm through for 1 minute, then serve immediately

Kitfo
Steak Tartare

Kitfo is eaten at the end of the meal to cleanse the palate. It is often served with *ayib*, an Ethiopian style cottage cheese, also known as *lab*. This is served plain (mixed with a little parsley, lemon zest, salt and pepper) or seasoned as *ayib be gomen*, the previous recipe in this collection.

As *kitfo* is eaten raw try to get the best quality lean beef you can afford and ask your butcher to mince it finely. If you are buying pre-ground look for a dark red meat that has been well aged with low water and fat content.

50g butter	½ tsp ground ginger
½ tsp cayenne pepper	Salt and pepper
½ tsp chilli powder	700g freshly ground lean fillet steak or a piece of premium beef
½ tsp cardamom	

PREP:

1 Melt the butter, stir in the cayenne, chilli, cardamom, ginger and seasonings. Cook until fragrant

2 Allow the mix to cool

3 Mix well into the beef and serve with *ayib*

COOK:

1. If you prefer the *kitfo* cooked, fry it gently for about 5 minutes, stirring constantly. Serve with *ayib*

Kitfo is finely chopped seasoned meat. People who have been to Ethiopia and have tried it there will always have it raw; those who have not usually ask for it medium. It is much better raw. If it is cooked it is like tibs and you lose some of the flavour.

A Chinese Kitchen

Introduction to Chinese Cuisine

The Chinese were great traders and explorers long before Marco Polo set sail across the world's oceans. Local ingredients were quickly complemented by new foods: wheat, sheep and goats were introduced from the westernmost parts of Asia and traded by nomads and merchants across the lands. During the Han and T'ang periods, fruit and vegetables were imported from central Asia. Peanuts and root vegetables, such as sweet potatoes, followed during the Ming dynasty.

Each region holds its own gourmet treasures. China's cuisine is one of the world's most popular but the food most foreigners recognise comes from the southern Canton region. Its location on the South China Sea means that it has had most contact with the outside world, trading with Asia, the Middle East and Europe. Cantonese people have also travelled the farthest, bringing their cuisine with them. The warmer climate and bountiful land and sea in the south proffer a wide variety of vegetables and rice, and an abundance of high quality sea-food and fish, which are all enjoyed daily. The fertility of this region has allowed Cantonese cooks to develop dishes to suit all tastes at all prices. From simple congee to roast goose and exquisite lobsters, the best ingredients are cooked minimally to bring out their natural flavours. A touch of garlic, a little ginger and spring onion fried in peanut oil and scattered over steamed fish or prawns are typical delicacies.

The north of China, historically populated by nomads who kept cattle and sheep, is a world away from this wealth: open fires on most street corners, hawkers cooking the finest, freshest beef and lamb on simple skewers; stockpots boiling with root vegetables, meat and warming spices. It remains a predominantly simple, robust cuisine, flavoured with garlic, ginger, onions – not to mention the infamous soy sauce.

The cuisine of central and western China can be grouped under the umbrella of Szechuan cooking. The highly spiced and aromatic dishes of this region are flavoured with what we know as five spices: equal parts of the local Szechuan pepper – a fragrant, woody pepper that is said to heat from the sinuses down and makes your eyes water – star anise, cinnamon, cloves and fennel seed. Dried and fresh red chilli are also used in abundance as the regional palate seems to crave hot food. Nevertheless, this is the only region to serve appetisers and congee as cold dishes, perhaps as a result of their dryer, warmer climate.

The eastern Hokkien region is reputed to have the most visually indulgent cuisine. Meats are often served braised and dyed bright red. Poultry and fish are cooked in thick, dark soy sauces in stark contrast to their white flesh. This region comes under the Shanghai culinary umbrella and the beautiful lotus plant is used liberally: the leaves as a vegetable, the seeds as a seasoning, and the flowers as decoration. The local, heady Shaoxing rice wine is used to add depth of flavour to the dishes and to accompany them. To counteract the richness of the foods and alcohol, jasmine scented green tea flows freely. It originated in this area before spreading all over the world.

Historically, frugality has been a key factor in the development of Chinese cooking methods. Frequent shortages of fuel have led to swift, efficient methods of cooking. Stir frying and steaming are the most common. They also have the advantage of maximising taste and retaining the most nutrients. Roasting was left to restaurants and other professional establishments. What better invitation to luxury and indulgence than to have slow roasted birds and meat hanging in your window. Perhaps not something you should try at home.

Flavours of a Chinese Kitchen

China is such a large country that its regional cuisines are highly distinctive but there are some elements common to all regions. The ingredients most Chinese cooks begin with – garlic, ginger and spring onion. The condiments – soy, oyster sauce and rice wine vinegar – and the characteristic herbs and spices used everywhere – coriander, star anise, Szechuan pepper, and chilli – can all be classed as typical Chinese flavours. It is extremely important to Chinese cooks to enhance and balance the four central flavours in food: sweet, bitter, salt, and sour. This is not just done in each dish, as with sweet and sour sauce, but in each meal. Balancing these four elements is the key to successful Chinese cuisine.

Chinese food is seen by many as rich and oily because we in the West are used to seeing hawker-style fried noodles and restaurant, sizzling and meat dishes. These are not typical of Chinese home cooking, where the emphasis is placed on rice – most commonly white rice and jasmine rice – served with a delicate balance of steamed, braised, baked and grilled foods. Cooks strive for harmony in aesthetics, smell, taste, and texture to ensure that the unique features of each dish are highlighted, contrasted and balanced. It is very important to retain the natural state of the ingredients. Fast stir frying in very little oil with pre-prepared and perhaps even pre-blanched ingredients keeps both colour and texture as natural as possible.

Any ingredients that cannot be cooked and eaten immediately are preserved by drying and pickling. This not only minimises waste, provides easy storage options, guarantees a source of food during times of shortage, but also intensifies the flavour of the food. The new texture and colour these foods take on often add another dimension to the dishes in which they are used.

You will find dried Chinese mushrooms and sausage in every Chinese store cupboard. There might also be dried seafood such as shrimp, scallops and abalone.

One of the most famous Chinese preserved foods is the 'thousand-year-old egg', also known as the century egg or preserved egg. These are duck or chicken eggs that have been coated in a mix of clay, ash salt, lime and tea, wrapped in rice husks and buried, i.e. stored in the dark for a few months rather than years. The yolk goes hard and forms a ball of dark and pale green swirls; the white turns a translucent cola brown colour. They can be eaten raw or boiled and are often served with steaming bowls of congee or pickled ginger – an acquired taste.

The Chinese place food at the heart of society. The normal greeting, "Have you eaten yet?" instead of "Hello" reflects its status. It is no surprise then that ingredients are held in high esteem, often representing the most important facets of life. Mushrooms, for example, represent prosperity because of their blooming nature and shape. Bamboo grows so fast that it too represents prosperity, also reflected in the golden hue of the shoot. Because of their abundance, lotus seeds represent fertility, as does rice. Long noodles mean long life so cutting them brings bad luck. Anything round, like the moon or the sun, is perceived as perfect, so melons, apples, grapes and oranges are often given as gifts. Spring rolls represent the shape of the early Chinese currency, so filling them with an abundance of bean sprouts for new growth will surely guarantee new money! Green vegetables are eaten in great quantities for they, too, represent seasons of plenty. The Chinese language is full of food metaphors: fish, for example, is most auspicious and brings good fortune because of its association with the word *yu* meaning 'extra' or 'abundance'. So if you eat fish your fortune will be abundant.

Perhaps because of the importance of food to the Chinese there is little emotional attachment to animals; most are seen as a good source of nourishment or flavour. Chinese markets are full of the freshest meat (i.e. still alive) and many seafood restaurants will have fish tanks at the front or back so that guests can choose what they would like to eat. Although this practice is not as welcome abroad as it is in China, it is still common. Taboo dishes, from monkey's brains to duck foetuses, are rarely seen abroad, but are still eaten by many mainland Chinese (overseas Chinese are less adventurous). More common on menus are cuts of meat that we in the West are unaccustomed to eating: chicken feet, chicken crests, duck's tongues and lots of tripe.

While we in the West drank mead and ale on a daily basis, in ancient China alcohol was regarded as a sacred liquid, used only when sacrificial offerings were made to Heaven, Earth or significant ancestors. Only appointed people – usually priests and senior adults – drank it in the form of liquors or *jiu* brewed from grain such as rice or millet. After the Zhou dynasty, alcohol became one of the Nine Rites and every dynasty since has placed great emphasis on its administration, even setting up special ministries to manage alcohol production and banqueting. Drinking alcohol in a more relaxed fashion is a relatively recent phenomenon, but now there are excellent beers such as Tsing Tao and Shanghai. The grape wine industry is growing slowly and some wines are creeping into our off-licences.

One cannot talk about the flavours of Chinese food without stressing the importance of what accompanies almost every meal: tea. Oolong, jasmine or green teas are most common abroad, but there are myriad varieties and blends of teas. Tea plays a role as medicine, as an offering, as the drink of the gods, and the drink of the people. Whatever its role, it joins food at the cornerstone of Chinese life.

Contents of a Chinese Store Cupboard

Ginger
Garlic
Star Anise
Five Spices
Coriander
Chilli – fresh, dried and powder
Lemon
Light and Dark Soy Sauce
Hoi Sin Sauce
Oyster Sauce
Plum Sauce
Chilli Sauce

Tomato Sauce
Fermented Black Beans
Spring Onions
Onions
Long Beans
Bamboo Shoots
Aubergine
Snow Peas
Corn
Leeks
Dried Mushrooms
Fresh Mushrooms – oyster, shiitake, cloud ear, wood ear
Water Chestnuts
Lotus Roots
Bean Sprouts

Chinese Green Vegetables:
Pak Choi, Gai Lan (Chinese Broccoli)
Chinese Cabbage, Kale

Peanuts
Cashew Nuts
Sesame Seeds
Sesame Oil
Vegetable Oil
Chinese Rice Wine
Sherry
Rice Wine Vinegar
Tofu
Eggs
Chicken Stock
Corn Flour
Won Ton Wrappers
Long Grain and Short Grain Rice
'Egg' Wheat Noodles
'Glass' Mung Bean Noodles
Fine and Thick Rice Noodles
Dried Scallops
Dried Prawns

Lessons learnt along the way...

Balance and harmony are two of the three most important features in Chinese life; cuisine is the third. The way your home is set up and decorated brings positive and negative energy into your life, just as the way you eat brings positive and negative energy into your body. Cooking generally follows the yin and yang principles, yin being cooling and yang being warming. These were developed to help people balance their diets and choose cooking styles. Each meal comprised only one dish prepared by any one method: yin dishes were boiled, poached or steamed; yang dishes were deep-fried, roasted or stir-fried.

If you saw any Oriental doctor, or any good grandmother for that matter, they would recommend a change in diet to sort out your ailments. If you had a cold you might be exposed to too many 'yin' or cooling forces so they would recommend 'yang' or warming ingredients such as ginger and chicken as well as herbal teas and spices.

Balance and harmony affect the foods served in each region. For example, in the cooler, humid south congee is usually served hot and savoury with ingredients such as roasted meats and century eggs; while in the north it is served sweet and cold with lily bulb flower and honey water, which are especially good for replenishing the skin and for balancing dryness and heat.

Chinese meals served at home are balanced not only by ingredient but by cooking method. Steaming and braising are more common than deep-frying and roasting:

The food we eat at home is not the same as the food we serve to customers; those dishes would be too rich and fragrant, too powerful to eat every day. The tastes I grew up with were rather simple. I suppose you might say that the traditional home-cooked food is blander; typically we prefer steamed dishes, especially fish and seafood with a touch of ginger or garlic and that's it.

Dishes should complement each other in appearance, flavour and texture. Each dish should have a different main ingredient and may be cooked using different techniques. This may sound complicated but it is as simple as avoiding three fried vegetables with roast meat; you would probably boil one, mash one, and roast the third.

Rice is the main component of most Chinese meals; in fact the word for rice, fan, is the same as the word for food. In order to get the balance right for everyday Chinese dining, think of meat as an accompaniment or flavouring that complements your main rice or noodle dish. General guidelines are that animal produce should constitute no more than one third of any meal and this ratio is a good basis for choosing Chinese food both at home and in a restaurant. Rather than three rich meat dishes with fried rice, as is common practice in the West, the Chinese would choose three rice or vegetable dishes for each meat dish.

Usually the number of dishes served corresponds to the number of diners, unless the number of diners is an unlucky number (4 or 7 in China). If there are four diners, three or five dishes are served; if seven, then six or eight dishes, which are accompanied by rice or noodles and a soup. The ingredients of the soup are often chosen for their medicinal purposes, and soup is considered an important part of the meal. Rather than being served as a starter it is drunk either throughout the meal, or just before dessert to cleanse the palate, the heat of the broth helping to dissolve any fats or grease in the food and thus further aiding digestion.

Although the service of a meal at home is relaxed with all the platters served at the same time and shared among family and guests, each helping themselves, there are rules of etiquette and behaviour that highlight the gweilo's (an affectionate term for 'foreign devil') ignorance.

You should slurp any noodles served in soup; this allows air into the mouth, which cools the noodles and helps the palate distinguish the subtle flavours of the soup, just as a vintner tastes wine. If tea is served with the meal, you always serve those around you before serving yourself and tap the table twice with your middle fingers to say thank you when someone pours for you. Thankfully the socially acceptable method of eating rice is to bring the small bowl close to one's mouth and scoop the rice into it, rather than try to pick it up grain by grain.

One endearing custom is to wait for the elders or more senior members at the table to raise their rice bowl as a gesture for the rest of the table to commence eating. In addition, we as more junior members at the table, normally offered the better parts of the meat/dishes to elders as a sign of respect.

The reason that the Chinese eat with chopsticks dates back to the influence of the philosopher Confucius, who believed that in the matter of advancing the 'civilisation' of the Chinese people, instruments of killing should be banned from the dinner table. Thus knives were restricted to the kitchen where they would be used to prepare the food into bite size pieces so nothing had to be cut at the table. There are superstitions associated with chopsticks too. If you find an uneven pair at your table setting, it means you are going to miss a boat, plane or train. Dropping chopsticks will inevitably bring bad luck, as will laying them across each other. You should also avoid putting your chopsticks end up in your rice: this is an insult as it makes them look like the incense sticks placed in sand at the temple when praying to the dead or the gods.

Foods that mark special occasions have special significance:

To celebrate people's birthdays they eat noodles, indicating longevity. For older relatives you are supposed to give 'perfect' round fruits like peaches and melons. For weddings there are lots of dates, peanuts and chestnuts that symbolize fertility, as well as rice, of course. This is to wish that the couple will be blessed with a baby soon. If you go away you'll often be sent off with dumplings, and on your return you will have lots of noodles.

Christmas is celebrated in most homes but with a distinctly Asian twist:

We tried turkey one year but found it too tough and bland and reverted to our lobsters, prawns and squid and now our neighbours want to join us for Christmas lunch because they love the way we served the lobsters.

Celebratory banquets are lavish affairs, usually a feast for the eyes as well as the stomach. Vegetables are carved into intricate sculptures or fishermen or dragons. Food is sliced and arranged to look like animals or flowers. Each dish is brightly coloured and complemented with an array of garnishes. At home, however, celebratory food is not always what you expect:

Because my mother is a Buddhist, Chinese New Year for us was not about indulging in prime cut meats and decadent sweets. From morning to evening we would have 'monks' food' – soups, salads, stir fried bamboo shoots, water chestnuts, mushrooms with black fungus and seaweed. Lots of small dishes to share that would leave what the Chinese call a 'clear palate'.

And perhaps a clearer conscience too; no need for the usual Western New Year dietary resolutions.

Recipes

Siu Mai
Pork and Prawn Dumplings with Chilli Dipping Sauce

Qing Zheng Yu
Steamed Sea Bass with Spring Onion, Ginger and Soy

Hai Wong
Empress Crabs

Char Sui
Roasted Barbecue Style Pork Fillet

Rou Yu Hsiang
Spicy Aubergine and Pork Hot Pot

Mut Tong Lat Jiuw Ji
Honey Chilli Chicken

Ng Heong Ngap
Braised Duck with Five Spice

Chow Choi
Stir Fried Green Vegetables with Garlic and Ginger

Doong Goo, Mook Yee, Chow Ngau
Stir Fried Beef and Three Mushrooms

Yangzhou Chow Fan
Yangzhou Style Fried Rice

Laigi Geng Suigo
Lychee and Ginger Sorbet

Mut Tow
Honey Walnuts

Siu Mai [Pork and Prawn Dumplings with Chilli Dipping Sauce]

Siu Mai

Pork and Prawn Dumplings with Chilli Dipping Sauce

Dim sum are served for early lunch on Saturdays and Sundays. Most Chinese families go to restaurants for their *dim sum*. It's a great chance for all the family to eat together and pick and choose their favourite dishes. The *dim sum* are brought round on trolleys loaded with huge varieties of steamed, fried and baked dishes that are offered by the waitresses as they go past. However, *dim sum* are very simple to make and many people prepare them at home and serve them as appetisers or snacks. *Won ton* wrappers can be found in most supermarkets and Chinese delicatessens. They are a great thing to have in the cupboard as they are so versatile. You can fill them with a teaspoon of almost anything, savoury or sweet, steam them as below, fry them or serve them in soup. The variations are so simple that you will find three recipes in one below:

Makes 16

16 wonton wrappers	2 tsp cornflour
For the filling:	Pinch of salt
200g raw prawns	Black Pepper
1 large spring onion	For the dipping sauce:
4cm ginger	1 red chilli
200g minced pork	3 or 4 stems fresh coriander
1 tbsp light soy sauce	2 tbsp sesame oil
1 tbsp rice wine vinegar	2 tbsp light soy sauce
1 tsp sesame oil	2 tbsp rice wine vinegar

PREP:

1 Peel, de-vein, clean and finely chop prawns

2 Chop spring onion

3 Peel and grate the ginger

4 Mix all the ingredients for the filling in a bowl

5 Prepare the sauce by deseeding and finely chopping the chilli and coriander, then mix them with the oil, soy sauce and vinegar

COOK:

- STEAM:

1. Prepare your surface by dusting with a little flour
2. Place a heaped teaspoon of the filling in the centre of the wonton wrapper
3. Dampen the edges of the wrappers with water and gather the sides of each wrapper around the filling in a ball shape leaving the centre of each dumpling unwrapped
4. Oil the bottom of a steamer and steam for about 6-8 minutes, or until the filling is cooked and the wrappers are soft
5. Serve straightaway with a dipping sauce

- FRY:

1. Prepare your surface by dusting with a little flour
2. Place a heaped teaspoon of the filling in the centre of each wrapper
3. Dampen the edges of the wrappers with water and gather all the corners around the filling, moulding each wonton so that there is no exposed filling and the air has been squashed out
4. Deep fry in hot oil until golden brown and crisp
5. Drain the wontons on absorbent paper before serving

- SOUP:

1. Prepare your surface by dusting with a little flour
2. Place a heaped teaspoon of the filling in the centre of each wrapper
3. Prepare as for fried dumplings
4. Simmer for about 5 minutes in boiling chicken stock. For added flavour you could add a little shredded spring onion and Chinese leaf, and a dash of rice vinegar and light soy sauce

Qing Zheng Yu [Steamed Sea Bass with Spring Onion, Ginger and Soy]

Qing Zheng Yu

Steamed Sea Bass with Spring Onion, Ginger and Soy

Although to many Westerners it might seem that Chinese food is always covered in thick sauces and flavoured with powerful spices this is not accurate. And when it comes to fish this could not be further from the truth. Like the Japanese, the Chinese believe that the flavour of fish is so delicate that it should be served as simply as possible. For this reason it is cooked over steam, then garnished with the flavourings so as not to mask its taste. It is common and only too easy to overcook fish. People worry about getting sick if it is undercooked but as long as the fish is fresh there is little chance of this happening.

The Chinese word for fish is *yu*. The same pronunciation as the word for 'remain'. From this coincidence the Chinese developed a tradition of serving fish at celebrations and happy occasions: the fish (*yu*) served at the meal guaranteed that the happiness felt by the participants would remain (*yu*) for a long time. For celebrations and parties the Chinese serve fish whole. A headless, tailless fish is considered incomplete and unaesthetic. There is also a practical reason for leaving the fish intact: less juice escapes during the cooking process. When buying fish ask your fishmonger to trim off the dorsal and side fins, but for an authentic look and taste leave the head on.

1 large sea bass (or trout or grey mullet)	2 cloves garlic
2cm fresh ginger root	2 tbsp sesame oil
1 fresh red chilli	2 tbsp vegetable oil
4 spring onions	Drizzle of soy sauce
Salt and pepper	1 small handful of fresh coriander

PREP:

1 Cut the ginger into fine matchsticks

2 Deseed and cut the chilli into fine threads

3 Shred the spring onions into fine threads ensuring you use the green stems of the onion as well as the white bulb

4 Clean the inside and outside of the fish then season the stomach cavity lightly with a little salt and pepper

5 Take a knife and make diagonal slashes across each side of the fish about $\frac{1}{2}$ cm deep. This helps the flesh cook more easily and evenly

COOK:

1. Place the fish in the steamer, ensuring there is room around the edges for the steam to circulate

2. Steam for about 8-12 minutes, until the fish is just cooked through

3. Once cooked lift the fish delicately on to a serving dish and garnish with a little ginger, garlic, chilli and spring onions

4. Put the two oils quickly into a small pan and heat until it smokes. Immediately pour over the fish and flavourings. The heat of the oil will cook the ingredients allowing the aromas to escape and taking away any raw bitterness

5. Drizzle on the soy sauce, scatter with coriander and serve as soon as possible

This is my favourite dish to cook because it is easy yet so fresh and tasty!

Hai Wong

Empress Crabs

Crabs and seafood are a Cantonese speciality. The abundance of good seafood means that these dishes are regularly enjoyed by families at the dinner table.

Most people who buy crab here do so in packs or tins, a travesty of flavour compared to the beautiful simplicity of a fresh crab. You have one body shell in which to stuff the rice and use as the top decorative piece, the other crab is for the crab meat. Fresh spring onions give a fresher cleaner taste; they are added right at the end of cooking.

2 (large) crabs	Water
3cm fresh ginger root	1 tbsp oil
2 spring onions	1/2 tsp salt
100ml sherry	1/2 tsp sugar
1 tbsp light soy sauce	1 tbsp soy sauce
200g glutinous rice	

PREP:

1 Clean crabs thoroughly

2 Chop one of them into several pieces with a large knife or cleaver and crack the hardest pieces of the shell with a hammer

3 Keep the body of the second crab intact. Empty it out except for a rim around the inside which is essentially the 'fat' of the crab

4 Separate the top body shell from the claws and the rest of the crab. Crack the claws and remove the meat

5 Finely chop spring onions and grate the fresh ginger, mash them together and combine with the sherry and soy sauce

6 Add to the crab and leave to marinate for 30-40 mins

7 Wash the glutinous rice in several changes of water until the water runs clear

COOK:

1. Put the rice into a rice cooker or pan and pour over 1 litre of water. Cover and steam until cooked through and a little sticky. (If you are using dried scallops add them to the rice water and cook for at least 5 minutes)

2. Add enough water to the steamer so the level is high but not touching the base of the steam basket

3. Layer the crab pieces on a dish and pack down with sticky rice

4. Stuff some rice into the top crab shell. Press the intact crab into the top of the rice and throw over any remaining marinate with a further tablespoon of soy sauce, 1 tablespoon of oil, 1 teaspoon of salt and 1 teaspoon of sugar

5. Place the dish in a steamer, cover and cook for 35-40 minutes

6. Fluff the rice a little to loosen and serve, garnished with spring onions

My parents also use dried scallops (6) for this dish. You need to prepare it a bit by boiling some water and placing the 6 scallops into a small bowl, fill with water and let it soak for 30 minutes before packing into the rice, it adds a delicate flavour to the dish.

Char Sui
Roasted Barbecue Style Pork Fillet

The pork fillet takes on a delicious caramel coating so it becomes slightly crisp on the outside but wonderfully soft in the centre. It can be chopped and used a a filling for *char sui bao* (barbecued meat buns), a popular Chinese lunch or snack and my favourite *dim sum*. The marinate would traditionally have some red dye in it giving it that restaurant look but synthetic food colourings do nothing to enhance the real beauty of ingredients and dishes, so I prefer not to include them.

This is a good meat dish to prepare on its own as a more Western style meal, accompanied by a few lightly steamed green vegetables and a little fluffy white rice.

1 shallot	1 tbsp brown sugar
1 clove of garlic	2 tsp sesame oil
2 tbsp soy sauce	1 tsp cinnamon
2 tbsp rice wine vinegar (or dry sherry)	1 lean pork fillet
2 tbsp clear honey	Szechuan peppers for garnish (optional)

PREP:

1 Roughly chop shallot and garlic

2 Combine with soy sauce, vinegar or sherry, honey, sugar, sesame oil and cinnamon in a large bowl

3 Add the pork and leave to marinate for an hour in the refrigerator, turning the meat occasionally. If you can leave it overnight so much the better

COOK:

1. Lift the fillets out of the bowl and place on a wire rack over a roasting pan. Keep the liquid for basting

2. Roast in a preheated moderate oven at 180°C for 30 minutes or until tender, basting frequently with the juices

3. Slice the fillet into thin slices and slide onto a warmed dish to serve

Rou Yu Hsiang
Spicy Aubergine and Pork Hot Pot

This is a real homey dish, one for those cold winter nights. The Chinese love pork and eat a lot of it at home. Aubergines take on a really smooth soft and almost silky texture when they are cooked slowly with the rice wine and stock. If you can find them, baby aubergines look and taste better in this dish. They are a little sweeter than the larger version and pack a little more flavour into their small shape. In addition, unlike the larger ones, they do not need to be salted to remove the bitterness of the flesh, thus saving time and effort. This is the sort of dish that is delicious reheated the next day as the flavours develop and the ingredients break down even more.

2 cloves of garlic	1 fresh chilli (or 1½ tsp chilli powder)
2cm ginger	1 heaped tsp five spice
5 small Chinese/baby aubergines (or 1 large aubergine)	2 tbsp dark soy
	250g minced pork
Sea salt	50ml rice wine
Vegetable, seed or peanut oil	500ml Chinese style chicken stock (or normal stock)
3 star anise	Sesame oil

PREP:

1 Peel and slice garlic and ginger

2 If you are using baby aubergines simply quarter lengthways. If you are using a large aubergine cut it into thick chips and salt liberally with sea salt, wait 20 minutes then rinse and dry

COOK:

1. Heat some oil in a hot wok or pan; add garlic, ginger, star anise, chilli and five spice and fry until aromatic

2. Add the pork mince and brown

3. Add the aubergine and fry a little to caramelise the outside

4. Add the rice wine and boil off the alcohol, which should take about 5 minutes

5. Add the stock and soy sauce; reduce the heat and simmer for 45 minutes to 1 hour until the pork and aubergines are really soft

6. Season with salt, pepper and sesame oil, and serve

Mut Tong Lat Jiuw Ji
Honey Chilli Chicken

This is a great example of a simple Szechuan dish: the hot chilli is balanced with the sweet honey. You can make this without the crisp coating of flour and the initial frying for a lighter dish by simply browning the meat before adding the chicken and frying it with the ginger and onion but I love the crunchiness the flour gives, and texture should be an important factor when planning a meal. Because these flavours are not so 'exotic' I prepare this for friends who love Chinese take-aways, want to diversify their cuisine at home but are not sure where to start.

4 chicken breasts or 1 joint per person	2 tbsp honey
Flour for dusting	Splash of water
Salt and pepper	Chilli sauce (or 3 fresh chillies, a little vinegar, a drop of water and 1 tbsp sugar)
2cm ginger	
2 spring onions	Juice of ½ lemon
Oil for deep frying	3 tbsp soy sauce

PREP:

1 Remove skin from chicken and slice breast into bite-size pieces

2 Season the flour with salt and pepper and roll the chicken in it, coating well

3 Finely chop the ginger

4 Shred the spring onions using the green stalks as well as the white onion bulbs

COOK:

1. Heat the oil and deep fry chicken pieces, in batches if necessary, until golden brown and cooked through. This will take about 6-8 minutes

2. Drain and dry on kitchen paper

3. Heat a tablespoon of oil in a wok or large pan

4. Fry the ginger and the white of the spring onion until they are caramelised, then add the honey, chilli sauce, water, lemon juice and soy sauce

5. Bring the sauce to the boil and allow to thicken for a few seconds

6. Stir in the fried chicken coating well, add the shredded green tops of the spring onion, and serve

Ng Heong Ngap
Braised Duck with Five Spice

A good stock is central to most cuisines and Chinese is no exception. It is used in soups, to lift stir frys, to add aroma to steamed buns, and in slow cooked stews. The rule of thumb is that it should be clear and golden. It is usually made with a mixture of mainly chicken but also pork bones and a few prawn shells wrapped in muslin. It is lighter than French-style stocks as it cooks for a couple of hours rather than sitting and slowly reducing for seven or eight hours. You get all the meaty flavour but it is fresher and less gelatinous.

This is a dense, dark dish, most impressive when served with perfectly steamed, fluffy white rice. The spices and the delicious dried Chinese mushrooms add an earthy autumnal depth of flavour to the sauce.

Serves 6

1 large duck (or 6 portions)	500ml chicken stock or water and stock cubes
3 cloves garlic	220g (small can) water chestnuts
5cm ginger	
2 tsp five spice	220g (small can) bamboo shoots
A handful of dried Chinese mushrooms	6 shallots
1 tbsp cornflour (or plain flour)	Sugar (to taste)
Splash of oil	Salt and pepper
2 tbsp dark soy sauce	1 tbsp sesame oil (to taste)
Generous splash of rice wine (or pale dry sherry)	

PREP:

1 Joint the duck into serving size pieces

2 Crush garlic and ginger and marinate the duck pieces with this and the five spice in a bag or bowl for at least 1 hour

3 Soak the Chinese mushrooms in hot water for 15-20 minutes, drain and slice

4 Roll the seasoned duck in cornflour

COOK:

1. Heat a little oil in a pan and brown the duck pieces a couple at a time cooking off the garlic and ginger at the same time. Remove from the pan

2. Drain the oil and duck fat from the pan and add soy sauce, rice wine or sherry, and stock; bring to the boil

3. Put all the duck back into the pan and reduce the heat to simmer for 1 1/2 hours or until the duck is tender, skimming off any scum or excess fat from the top of the stew

4. Add sliced Chinese mushrooms, drained water chestnuts and bamboo shoots; season with extra soy, sugar, salt, pepper, and sesame oil. Simmer for 20 minutes

5. Serve with steamed rice

Chow Choi
Stir Fried Green Vegetables with Garlic and Ginger

Vegetables cooked in this style are crisp and keep their colour. The cooking time is short so the flavours as well as the vitamins and minerals are all retained.

3 cloves of garlic	500g broccoli
1cm fresh ginger	190ml chicken or vegetable stock
2 onions	3 tbsp oil
1 large bunch kale	
½ Chinese cabbage	

<u>PREP:</u>

1 Roughly chop the garlic and grate the ginger

2 Prepare all the vegetables by chopping into bite size pieces: quarter the onions, slice the kale and cabbage so that the stalks and leaves are separate, and trim the broccoli. Set aside the stalky pieces; these will to be cooked first

3 If using stock cubes, boil water in a kettle and allow to cool slightly before making the stock. Set aside in a jug

COOK:

1. Heat the oil in a wok, add garlic and ginger and wait for the aroma

2. Once this has hit add the onion and stalky vegetable pieces, stir fry, coating all the vegetables in the hot oil for about 1 minute

3. Add the remaining vegetables and toss lightly

4. Add the stock and bring to the boil

5. Cover and cook until the vegetables are tender. This should take about 3 minutes

6. Remove the lid and allow any remaining water to evaporate, stirring occasionally. Serve

One of my favourite vegetables for this is kale. The touch of garlic makes it easy to polish off a full plate of these greens.

Doong Goo, Mook Yee, Chow Ngau [Stir Fried Beef and Three Mushrooms]

Doong Goo, Mook Yee, Chow Ngau

Stir Fried Beef and Three Mushrooms

The Chinese eat a much wider variety of mushrooms than we in the West. Despite the introduction of oyster, chanterelle and porcini mushrooms to the mainstream market people usually reach for the safe, pre-packaged punnets of white button mushrooms. Such a shame, as the varieties really are diverse in flavour and texture adding new dimensions to any dish. The Chinese mushroom, also called *shiitake*, black mushroom or forest mushroom (not to be confused with the European wild mushrooms) are the most widely used mushrooms in Chinese cooking. They have a delicious flavour and easily absorb the taste of other ingredients. Their fleshy caps are dense but their stems can be tough and so are sometimes used for flavouring before being discarded. They are sold fresh or dried and are a good item for the store cupboard as they last for up to a year. A few can be added to any stock or soup for extra flavour. Oyster mushrooms are fan-shaped with white flesh and a grey-brown exterior. They are soft and can be used raw to add a peppery, robust flavour. This mellows when they are cooked making them an excellent addition to casseroles, soups or stir frys.

Wood ear fungi, also known as cloud ear or tree ear mushrooms, are popular in Szechuan cooking. Their flavour is not as distinct but they have a wonderful texture. The brownish beige flesh is smooth, firm and crunchy. They are often added to clear broths at the last minute or used in braising.

300g beef (sirloin or rump are good)	5cm ginger
A large handful of dried Chinese mushrooms	1 tbsp sesame oil
	1 tbsp light soy sauce
50g wood ear (or chestnut) mushrooms	Peanut Oil (or other seed oil) for frying
50g oyster mushrooms	2 spring onions
2 cloves of garlic	100ml oyster sauce

PREP:

1 Rinse the dried Chinese mushrooms and wood ear mushrooms and soak for 30 minutes in hot water

2 Wash them quickly in cold water and remove any sticky bits

3 Slice all the mushrooms

4 Peel and chop the garlic and ginger and the white part of the spring onion, setting aside the green part

5 Slice the beef and rub it with sesame oil and soy sauce

COOK:

1. Heat the peanut oil in a wok until very hot, add the garlic, the white part of the spring onion and ginger; fry off with the Chinese mushrooms

2. Add beef and stir fry quickly then add the other mushrooms, sauté, and toss in the oyster sauce. Keep turning the mushrooms and beef so they do not overcook but get coated in sauce. Serve immediately garnished with a little chopped green spring onion

Yangzhou Chow Fan
Yangzhou Style Fried Rice

Fried rice is usually made with leftover rice from previous meals that is re-heated in a wok with oil and flavoured with some egg and any other ingredients to hand. In fact if you are stir frying rice from scratch make sure it cools before frying it so that the grains form a dry shell; otherwise you will have a starchy, mushy mess rather than fluffy rice.

175-225g long grain rice	2 spring onions
3-4 dried shiitake mushrooms	Pinch of salt
100g peeled prawns	50g green peas
100g cooked ham or pork	3 tablespoons sunflower oil
2-3 eggs	1½ tablespoons light soy sauce

PREP:

1 Prepare the rice as for steamed rice (see opposite) and allow it to become cold

2 Soak the Chinese mushrooms in boiling water for 20 minutes. Drain, discard the hard stalks, and dice the caps

3 Cut the prawns into 2-3 pieces if large

4 Dice the ham or pork

5 Beat the eggs slightly with a fork and about half of the spring onions, finely chopped

COOK:

1. Heat 1 tbsp of the oil in a wok or frying pan and scramble the eggs. Season with a pinch of salt. Remove from the pan and set aside

2. Heat the remaining oil and stir fry the mushrooms and peas with the prawns and ham or pork

3. Add the cooked rice and soy sauce, stirring to separate each grain of rice. Finally add the scrambled eggs, breaking them into small pieces. Add the remaining spring onions as a garnish and serve hot

This is a student's staple; it takes no time at all and makes a meal in one step. 'Overnight rice' is the best kind to use, i.e. leftovers. Make sure the wok is really, really hot. This is crucial. You can add prawns, peas, pretty much anything you want to this

Pak Fan
Perfect Steamed Rice

The Chinese eat their rice plain, usually steamed. Most Chinese families have a rice steamer that comes with a measuring cup. All they have to do is throw in a cup of rice and two of water, close the lid, turn it on and the rest is done. If you don't have a rice steamer, ensure you use the same glass/cup/bowl for measuring both water and rice so you have twice as much water as rice. This should ensure fluffy steamed rice every time.

| 1 cup of long grain rice | ½ tsp salt |
| 2 cups of water | |

PREP:

1 Wash the rice so that most of the starch is removed and the water runs fairly clear

2 Put the rice in a large saucepan and add double the volume of water. Add the salt and stir

COOK:

1. Bring the water to the boil rapidly with the pan uncovered until steam holes appear in the rice. Cover and turn the heat right down

2. Allow the rice to cook gently until it is tender. This will take about 15-20 minutes

3. Remove from the heat and allow the rice to stand for a few minutes with the lid on

4. Use a fork to fluff the grains of rice and separate them before serving

TIP:
Freeze rather than refrigerate any unused rice. It is more hygienic and is perfect for fried rice when you want a quick, healthy meal.

Laigi Geng Suigo
Lychee and Ginger Sorbet

Chinese food has a reputation for being heavy on the stomach if you don't get the right balance of rice, tea and oily foods, so it is nice to finish the meal with something fresh and digestive. Stem ginger is very popular in Chinese cuisine and is often used as a topping for desserts or in baking but I love the syrupy tang it gives to this fresh sorbet. Lychees are sweet and intensely aromatic so rather than a hit of flavour it seems to grows on the palate. This can be made in the freezer, without an ice-cream machine. Provided you whisk it after a few stages to break up the ice crystals it will turn out perfectly.

2 cans lychees in syrup	3 tbsp stem ginger syrup
1 stem candied ginger	2 egg whites
1 lime	

PREP:

1 Drain the lychees and put the syrup aside

2 Put the fruit in a blender with the ginger, the grated rind of the lime, and a generous squeeze of lime juice

3 Mix this purée with the lychee syrup you had put aside and the stem ginger syrup. Freeze for 1 hour until slushy

4 Remove from the freezer and whisk to break the ice crystals

5 Whisk the egg whites until they are stiff. Fold into the mixture

6 Return to the freezer for another 2 hours until firm

We don't eat 'pudding' in the same way as Westerners do but on occasion we end our meal with a cleansing fruit sorbet or candied nuts. Lychees are one of the most delicate Asian fruits, fragrant and sweet, so they work really well combined with warming, sharp ginger.

Mut Tow
Honey Walnuts

You may think it odd to put soy sauce in a sweet dish but because of the honey and sugar a little salt in the form of soy sauce lessens the intensity and helps balance the dish. Dropping the nuts into hot oil cooks the caramel fast giving the nuts a really satisfying crunch. You will find that some caramel floats in the oil. This will burn unless you are on hand with a slotted metal spoon to scoop it out. Put it onto some greaseproof paper and crush it up later to use as a topping or garnish for cakes. When you spoon out the walnuts make sure that you separate them on the wire rack or they will be stuck together once the sugar cools. If you prefer not to deep fry then you can place the nuts on an oiled baking tray and cook them in a hot oven for 10 minutes but the walnuts and caramel remain chewy and make your teeth stick together. Some people like it that way!

Honey walnuts make a great snack but are especially delicious crushed and served warm on rich coconut ice cream or served as an alternative to chocolates with after-dinner coffee.

180ml honey	100g caster sugar
1 tbsp lemon juice	Groundnut oil for deep frying
1 tsp soy sauce	
250g walnut halves	

PREP:

1 In a bowl mix honey, lemon juice, and soy sauce

2 Add the walnuts and stir well to ensure they are completely coated in the mixture. Allow to marinate for at least 2 hours, stirring occasionally to ensure complete coating

3 Pour the sugar onto a large plate

4 Take the walnuts out, a spoonful at a time, and roll them in the sugar, making sure they are well coated and separated. Put on a clean, dry plate

COOK:

1. In a heavy-based pan heat about 200ml of oil. You need enough to just cover the walnuts

2. Drop them in in batches so that the temperature of the oil remains as constant as possible. Cook until deep golden brown, which takes about 1 minute

3. Drain well with a slotted spoon and place on a wire rack with baking paper below to protect any surfaces from the dripping caramel

Measurements and Conversions:

Glug = 10ml

Generous Glug = 20ml

1 Teaspoon = 5ml

1 Tablespoon = 15ml

American Cup = Approximately ½ Pint, 290ml
or10 Fluid Ounces

METRIC – IMPERIAL

Metric	Imperial
15 g	½ oz
30g	1 oz
55g	2 oz
85g	3 oz
110g	4 oz (¼ lb)
140g	5 oz
285g	10 oz
340g	12 oz (¾ lb)
450g	16 oz (1 lb)
900g	2 lb
2.3kg	5lb
4.5kg	10lb

LIQUID
1 Pint = 568ml or 20 fluid ounces
Average Bottle of Wine =750ml or 75cl
Average Glass of Wine = 100ml or 3.5 Fluid Ounces

LENGTHS

Metric	Imperial
1 cm	½ inch
2.5 cm	1 inch
5 cm	5 inch
20 cm	8 inch

OVEN TEMPERATURES
General Guide

Centigrade	Fahrenheit	Gas Mark
150	300	2 Cool
180	350	4 Slow*
200	400	6 Medium
230	450	8 Hot
250	480	9 Very Hot

* Slow cooking is best as it usually brings out the
flavours of ingredients much more effectively; this is
the optimum temperature for most home cooking

Index of Recipes

Grazie Mille, Motashakkeram, Thank You, Merci Beaucoup, Shukriya, Terima Kasih Banyak-Banyak, Südamlik Aitäh, Betam Amesgënallô, M Goi!

Thanks to my little Melting Pot of friends and family who have been on this great journey with me – we're here and it has been a pleasure.

My adorable husband Rob, without your constant support and encouragement these pages would be blank. Here's to a life less ordinary. I love you.

Shareen Chua and Ari Omar – Champers in the snow after mountain hikes in the Torres del Paine National Park – who would have thought it would lead to this! Thanks for all your boundless enthusiasm, great appetites and generosity. Your photos are fab. Thanks for lending me your kitchen and some posh plates for the shoots too. Congratulations on the birth of your beautiful son Zach.

Rebecca Dadson – a whirlwind of fun and enthusiasm, professionalism and passion. Thanks for your time, effort, advice, and agreeing to come on board in Covent Garden; nice one chick – here's to the bubble never bursting.

To all my lovely ladies many thanks for letting me grill you on your lives, hassle you for random bits of info at all hours, and convince you to pose for the camera – you're all beautiful:
Miss Caribbean – Sonia Nimley; Miss India – Meera Buhecha; Miss France – Rowena Lewis; Miss Estonia – Helen Hopper; Miss Iran – Pamela Clough; Miss China – Elisabeth Chan (Buffy); Miss Ethiopia – Mimi Tsion; and Miss Malaysia (Shareen Chua).

Thanks to Andreas Papadakis for believing in the concept and pushing to make a beautiful book when others were afraid to take the leap.

Thanks to Alexandra Papadakis for always being at the other end of the phone and keeping up the pace on production. It's been great fun working with you.

Mum and Dad for being so positive about my life choices and being so much fun to grow up with. Thanks for making me a global citizen with firm roots. Ti amo tantissimo.

Grazie mille a la mia famiglia Bergamasca: Per tutte le Natale insieme – per le patate della Nonna, le paseggiate con gelati in mano in Citta Alta, per Nonno, le Pasticcini da La Marianna tutti gli anniversari al Pianone, siete sempre nel mio cuore.

Thanks Clive and Kaja for the Estonian contingent and the rest of the Hopper clan for constant support – especially my big bro Christian, whose ribbing always keeps me focused. Love you all.

Lastly Helen Tillott – a friend indeed, thanks for believing in me and my ideas from the beginning. We've been on a great journey together. Thanks for all the selfless effort and encouragement you have put in, with words of wisdom and giggles along the way. I am so grateful. Thanks also to Phil (and Betty for the great eggs!).